As Far Back As I Can Remember

by Anna Diener Yoder

AS FAR BACK AS I CAN REMEMBER
By Anna Diener Yoder

International Standard Book Number

1-897373-11-2

Printed by WORD ALIVE PRESS
131 Cordite Road, Winnipeg, MB R3W 1S1
www.wordalivepress.ca

Printed in the United States of America

TABLE OF CONTENTS

Author's Notes

I write this book tucked full of childhood memories to show the reader that it is the "itty-bitty bits of this and that" of every day living that build character and instill spiritual thirst and hunger after God. I also write it to find myself in the little whimsical Amish girl of the past. My purpose is to give expression to that little Amish girl who had difficulty grasping the things going on around her, and I have striven to set these memories each into their proper setting.

Even from childhood I have had a desire to be a writer. However, Mama said writers and artists were lazy people who sat around writing stories and painting pictures instead of working. After I got married my seven babies kept me from my desire, but now that I'm a grandma, I realize that it is now or never! I love my family dearly and would not have chosen to have been born into another. Life without them would be dull, empty and barren. Basically I had a happy, carefree childhood, but full of many misconceptions that made me hard to live with. I'm thankful to God for placing me in the family he did. I wouldn't have wanted it any other way.

I also want to show the grace of God holding and cuddling me until the day of His grace arrived—whereby, at the age of twenty-six, God removed the ugly shreds of self-righteousness from my heart and drew me to Himself. It was a long journey from the belief that "Surely God wouldn't cast me into hell" to the realization that hell is exactly what I deserved. On that day God sent a flash of light and implanted HIS EVERLASTING RIGHTEOUSNESS within my soul.

~Anna Diener Yoder

Preface

I have striven to record the memories and feelings that keep popping up inside me of the little Amish girl that's still running around in there, her fears, her tears, her denseness, her misconceptions, her insecurities, as well as the securities and love in which she was wrapped. And so, I've stepped back inside to release those memories—memories that are so vivid and real that I still feel them. To my surprise I've found a release from many of my insecurities and have discovered that I've been wrapped in a mantle of LOVE.

I can truly testify that any love shown to a child, even though that child is too young to remember, is never lost. I have a special spot in my heart that will always be there for my daddy and for Uncle Obey's family. (That's my daddy's oldest brother; he's a generation older then my daddy.) Mother was sickly after I was born, and Daddy basically dressed, diapered, fed and cared for me. During harvest times, I spent many weeks in my Uncle Obey's home, cuddled and loved by a house full of girls. When I was twenty months old, the twins came along, so I continued on in Uncle Obey's household. I do not remember it. But oh, how deeply, even as an adult, I love that family! Down through the years, as I've infrequently mixed with these cousins (there are only fifty-some Diener cousins), they invariably tell me of the days I spent in their teenage home.

I was four years old when we left Illinois. Most of those memories are so vague I cannot write about them, but I recall plainly and clearly when we landed in the heart of the Allegheny Mountains of southwestern Pennsylvania. It was like a jolt that brought my memory to life...

Horses Pull Buggies

I sit on Daddy's knee in the buggy and cuddle deep into his arms. I'm mesmerized by the steady sway of the reigns and the clip-clap of the horse's hooves on the hard-packed dirt road. The baby twins are nestled comfortably in Mom's large lap. Sarah and Moses share the narrow bench behind us.

"Ouch!" Sarah cries as she scoots toward the corner behind Mom.

"Ouch!" I twist on Daddy's knee and peer into the dimness behind me. Moses's long arms and legs follow Sarah into her corner.

"Behave yourself," Mom says to Moses as she turns slightly toward him. I slide off Daddy's lap and reach up to grab the top edge of the buckboard in front of me. I stretch onto my tippy-toes and peer into the back end of the horse. I don't notice that I'm pressed between Daddy's and Mom's knees.

The tail of the horse rises slowly upward and slightly backward. My eyes grow big with wonder. The horse doesn't lose its trotting pattern as several large "fluckes" emerge from beneath the tail and drop to the ground. The tail lowers and the aroma is soon left behind. I crawl back into Daddy's lap and nestle securely into his arms.

When Daddy turns the horse into Uncle Obey's lane I get excited. By the time he pulls up to the hitching post our buggy is surrounded with eager teenage girls waiting to have a baby handed down to them. The twins quickly disappear out of Mom's lap, then I'm handed down into waiting arms. Sarah follows Mom into the house, and Moses runs into the barn to play with the boys while Daddy takes care of the horse.

When the long church service begins I nestle contentedly into Aunt Obey Annie's lap and finger the string of beads she's given me. I like the long slow German hymns sung out of the little black books. Soon after the preaching in High German begins, a large deep bowl of big round church cookies passes down our bench. They're for the babies and old folks. I nibble contentedly and soon the rise and fall of the German preaching fades into the background and I drop off to sleep.

Fragments of a Move

When I was four years old a great change came into my life, but I remember only a few fragments of the move from the flat fertile plains of Arthur, Illinois, to the beautiful, mountain rock-laden farm at the foot of Mount Davis, the highest peak in the Allegheny Mountains of Somerset County, Pennsylvania. Even so, it was the jolt that brought my memory to life.

In my mind I see two stock trucks being loaded in the large area between the house and the barn on our Illinois farm. Cattle and horses are loaded into one and equipment, furniture and barrels of household goods into the other. One truck leaves a day before the other. Our car follows the second truck, which contains the cattle.

Daddy has bought himself a new 1940 Chevrolet and has been visiting the Mennonite Church in the little town of Arthur. As a result, the Old Order Amish Church put the "Church Miting" on our family. That is what happens to people who do not keep the ordinances of the church. No one buys, sells or eats with them. Of course, I am not aware of this, but it is what helped my folks decide to move to Pennsylvania.

Early one morning before daybreak Daddy carries me to the car and places me in the seat behind him with the others, but I keep on sleeping. I awake when the car stops. Daddy is climbing up the side of the stock truck that's stopped in front of us.

"Everything is OK," Daddy says to Mom when he comes back into the car.

At my feet is a wooden crate. Inside are my most prized possessions—two cats! Somewhere in the West Virginia hills Daddy pulls off the road to let the cats go to the bathroom.

"Go fetch the cats," Daddy says to my oldest brother, Moses. Moses disappears into the woods. I hear him screeching, yelling, and chasing the cats deep into the forest.

"No! No!" I cry when Daddy pulls the car back onto the highway. "Don't leave the cats!" My heart breaks. I whimper and cry for hours. Mom and Daddy try to comfort me, but there is no consolation—no, not until weeks later when a small kitten is placed into my arms again.

The sun is setting and darkness is creeping over the mountain ranges when Daddy pulls off the hard road onto a long, dusty lane. I'm still "sniffling" about the cats. We go up, up and around, then across a flat plateau. Suddenly the lane takes a sudden dive downward, curving here and there among large boulders and trees. Down! Down! Down! Finally we come around a curve and a large flat plateau spreads out in front of us. In the darkening twilight I see a barn with a large brick house beyond. A tall hedge separates the house from the barn.

Daddy pulls up to the rose arbor entrance by the tall hedge. The two trucks are parked by the barn. We follow Mom and Daddy into the house. It is cold, damp and empty. I cry and hang onto Mom's big loose apron. I am cold, damp and hungry. Daddy goes to the basement and builds a fire in the big furnace.

"Annie, stop crying!" Mom scolds as she pushes me out of the way. She's digging through a large barrel one of the truck drivers has put into the kitchen. She's looking for a pot. But I can't stop crying. Daddy brings in Mom's little kerosene burner and a box full of supplies. Then he milks one of the cows. Soon a pot of "Blie" is bubbling on the burner. "Blie" is a plain hot milk pudding with brown sugar sprinkled over it. By the time our "Blie" is ready Daddy has found the little tin-topped table and a few crates for us to sit on. The wonderful "Blie" puts a warm glow in my stomach.

Epilogue:

Later I heard Daddy say that our move from Illinois was extremely hard on his cows and that they never produced well again.

ILLINOIS FARM HOUSE WITH CHICKEN COOP ON RIGHT

ILLINOIS FARM BARN

A Certain Shade of Yellow

"I'll have supper on the table by the time you come in," Mom says to Daddy as she leaves the barn with several empty milk buckets. We're settled on our new farm by now. It's late Saturday night and it's been a long hard day. Mom is tired, but there is still much to do before she can bathe her children and tuck them into bed.

"I don't like the little ones being left alone in the house while I help in the barn," Mom says to the large German Shepherd dog that is following her, "but it can't be helped now that the days are growing short and cold."

Mom steps into the basement door and stops in horror! NO! IT CAN'T BE—IT JUST CAN'T BE!

But yes, it is! Mom's brand new double-tub wringer washing machine stands with an uneven coat of dull yellow paint dabbed all over it. Then she notices yellow paint dabbed on the floor, walls and everywhere! In the far recesses of the basement stand the twins, still dabbing paint, they themselves well-covered with the dreadful dull yellow. What does Mom do? Well, she has a long, hard cry!

Mom had asked Daddy to give her old kitchen cupboard a new coat of paint. She wanted it to be the popular dull yellow everyone was putting into their kitchens.

"I don't like that homely *shise gail*," (the yellow color of newborn calf manure) Daddy said every time Mom talked to him about it. That made Mom mad. When Daddy finally found time to paint Mom's cupboard for her he brought it into the basement, but chore time came before he finished, so he laid the lid lightly on the can and placed the brushes on top.

Mom gets up from the stool she has flopped on and draws water from the hot reservoir above the furnace. She fills the large oblong galvanized tub, then undresses the twins and plops them into it. After drawing another bucket of hot water Mom begins scrubbing the paint off her new washing machine, the walls and the floor.

"Will my new washing machine ever be bright and shiny again?" Mom asks herself as she wipes away a few tears.

When everything is clean she turns back to the twins, who are happily playing in the sudsy tub. After a thorough scrub-down she takes them out and dries them with a towel. But alas, the backs of their legs and bottoms are plastered with a brand new coat of dull yellow paint. The twins have painted the bottom of the tub also!

What does Mom do? She has another long, hard cry, then she scrubs the tub and bathes the twins again.

The Mean Game

"I hate Mose," I sob.

"Now, Annie," Mom says, "you must not hate your brother. You cannot go to Heaven if you hate your brother! Besides, what will people think?"

"I hate him," I wail. I am perplexed. I love God and I want to go to Heaven, but the fact is I hate my brother! He's extremely mean and I'm afraid of him. I often dream he is killing me. It all started as a game.

"Let's play a new game," Moses says to Sarah, my older sister, as he ducks under the grape arbor where she and I are playing house. "Today I'll be mean to you and tomorrow I'll be meaner. Each day I'll get meaner and meaner. Let's see how mean I can get without you telling Mom."

ERLA AND A DUCK UNDER THE GRAPE ARBOR.

Soon the "mean game" spreads to include me and then the twins. Mom and Daddy try to persuade Moses to be kind, but instead, he intensifies his meanness. They scold and whip while he rolls on the floor and laughs. But we little kids, we cry. Mom and Daddy do everything they can, but Moses only gets meaner.

I shake in terror and feel paralyzed every time his shrill shrieks erupt into the air. Moses' whoops and hollers can be heard a long way off. Tears run down my face as the others and I scatter to hide. We hide among the calves and behind cows that are lying down chewing their cud. We crawl into hay mangers, burrow into straw stacks, and crawl under chick hovers. We hide in all the various spots that only a large, dark barn can sport.

One day after the folks have gone to town we huddle in the locked upstairs bathroom. We can't go along to town—they need room to bring the supplies home. The bathroom is safely located on the third floor above the basement entry. Suddenly Moses' face appears at the window. Fear fills my bosom and paralyzes my hands and legs as I fumble in fright with the others to unlock the bathroom door. We stumble down the stairs as Moses' long legs come leaping up the stairs. It's as though he has a dozen arms and legs thrashing in every direction. By the time the folks arrive home the tall ladder has disappeared from the window.

All through my childhood I struggle with "He that loveth not his brother, loveth not God." It is a great mystery to me. I love God, and want to go to Heaven, and yet, I fear and hate my brother.

I Love the Name Mary

I'm crying. I'm crying very hard. My heart is breaking. I should be happy like everyone else is. My new baby sister has just arrived, and I was excited along with my brothers and sisters—that is, until I hear that her name is not Mary! But why not? Mary is such a pretty name.

I don't know exactly why I love the name Mary, but I love it. Maybe it's because of Mary, the mother of Jesus. All my imaginary friends, as well as my rag doll, are named Mary.

During the last few weeks there's been much talk about naming our new baby.

"Name her Mary," I say.

"Annie, it may not be a girl," Mom says every time I talk to her about naming the baby Mary. I'm excited. I'm sure the baby will be a girl, and her name will be Mary!

Finally the baby arrives.

"It's a little girl!" Daddy announces when he comes home from the hospital.

"I have a new baby sister!" I yell run through the house. "Her name is Mary!" I tell everyone.

"Her name is Erla," Mom says when she and the new baby come home.

"Erla?" What a strange sounding name!

"It isn't pretty like Mary," I whine. I crawl up on the big old maroon over-stuffed chair and begin to cry.

"Annie," Mom says every few minutes from her bed in the corner of the living room, "stop crying!"

"Annie!" Mom's voice gets sterner. "I said, stop crying!"

"Annie!"

"Annie!"

Daddy comes to my chair, picks me up, and holds me. He speaks tenderly to me, but I cannot stop crying.

"Annie," Mom finally says, "the next baby we will name Mary." I dry my tears and take my turn holding my new baby sister, Erla.

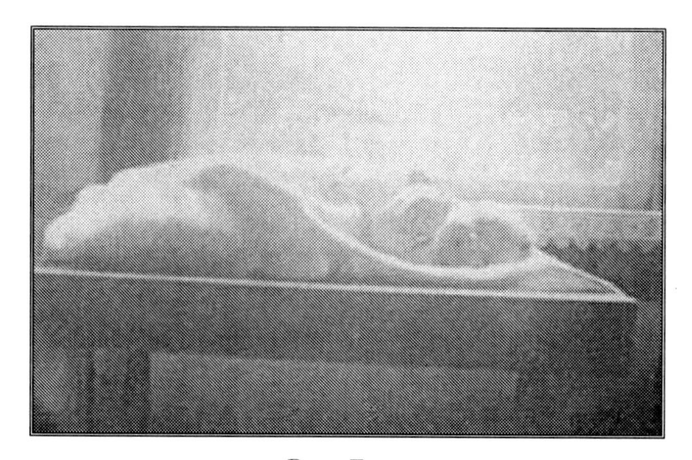

BABY ERLA

Epilogue:

However, there never is a next baby, or a Mary—no, not until my own little daughter Mary comes into my life.

The Twins and Me

"Can you tell which two are the twins?" Mom asks the stranger. If Mom has dressed Lydie and me alike we are chosen. If Lydie and I are not dressed alike, Lester and I are chosen. If they know that the twins are a boy and a girl, but none of us are dressed alike, Lester and I are still chosen.

"Why don't I remember?" I whine to Mom as I wrap myself in her apron. "I don't remember when Lydie and Lester were born. They've always been here. It's always been the twins and me!"

"They are twenty months younger than you," Mom explains. "You're older."

"But I don't remember ever being bigger then them. We've always been the same size," I say. "Why can't I remember?"

"You are each different," Mom says. "Even the twins are not alike. Lester is chubby, with a light complexion and a crop of thick white hair."

"Lydie has dark hair and is beautiful. Everyone says so," I say. I feel a big ugly pout coming up out of the pit of my stomach and spreading across my face.

"But you're pretty too," Mom says. "God makes us each different. I know you're small for your age and light-complexioned, but your hair is darker than Lester's."

"But I'm not pretty like Lydie," I say as my chin drops to my chest.

"Pretty is as pretty does," Mom says as she lifts my chin and looks into my eyes.

I don't like it when Mom does that, and I don't like it when she lines us up in front of strangers. I wiggle, twist and turn as I pull a few loose strands of hair out from under my cap on my forehead and chew on them.

"Annie! Stop that," Mom says as she slaps my hand. "Hold still! Take the hair out of your mouth!"

The twins may not look alike, but they stick together. And that's where most of my trouble comes in. It's two against one and I usually trail behind them.

It is true, they somehow know the best way to do things, and we have lots of fun. What one twin doesn't think of, the other one does. It seems to me that they know the what's, when's and where's of everything. Even though I'm bossy and want my own way, I learn to follow behind and share in their fun. However, I usually make a big fuss—after all, I am the oldest and I should have some say in such important matters.

I'm Bashful

The summer before I entered school I walked four miles with my brother and sisters to attend the two-week summer vacation Bible School held in the local village. My arms remained tightly folded across my chest and my head down. No one could get a response from me. The first day the twins crawled out of their classroom window, jumped into the bushes below, and headed for home. If I had known, I'd have gone with them.

At age six I enter school. The first and second grades are in the same room, but I have a problem. I still do not understand English, so I do not utter a sound for two years. What are those strange blocks of paper taped above the long blackboard at the front of the room? Several times a day the teacher picks up a long stick and points to the blocks and the class makes funny sounds. There are a few other Amish children in the room, and they make the funny sounds, but I mind my own business and keep coloring the pictures the teacher gives me.

"I don't want to go to school!" I say to Mom each morning, "I want to color my pictures at home."

"Everyone has to go to school," Mom says. "Do you want your father sitting in jail like your Uncle Enos is?" Mom asks one day.

"No!" I exclaim as I wipe my eyes and follow the others out the door.

Sometimes the teacher comes home overnight with me, but that doesn't help. My little brother Lester takes over and chatters with the teacher all evening.

"Annie was a late talker in German too," I hear Mom tell the teacher, "and it's never been plain. But once she started talking she's never shut up. I guess she's making up for lost time." Mom and the teacher chuckle.

Even so, it is not until the twins join the classroom that I slowly begin to comprehend what school is all about.

I'm *Schtruwblich*

Mom is looking at my school pictures. Finely chewed hairs protrude from under the black head covering in several directions. The covering itself is crooked, the strings chewed and unevenly tied. There are several food spots on the apron. She sighs and looks at me.

"There is no denying it," she says, "it does look natural, but it certainly is not the way I sent you to school. Why didn't the teacher slick the hair back and straighten the cap? She could at least have tied the strings straight. What kind of mother will people think I am?"

That day Mom begins a campaign to break my hair-chewing habit. I soon discover that chewing my hair while I sit at my school desk is unprofitable. Somehow, Mom can always tell.

This isn't the first nervous habit Mom has helped me overcome. I clearly remember the day my new baby sister came to live at our house. Everyone had a turn holding her except me.

"Annie," Mom had said sternly, "stop crying. I meant every word I told you! You'll get to hold baby Erla as soon as you allow a scab to grow across the sore on the top of your head."

So now, instead of picking sores on my head I pull out strands of hair and chew them. But Mom has said that must stop too. So, the hairs I retrieve from under my black covering I twist round and round my pencil as I sit for long hours at my school desk. They break off at the roots. Mom notices that too.

"Annie," she says, "I'm chasing your nervous habit from one thing to the next. Aren't you ever going to grow up? What will people think?"

Then one day, as I'm twisting a strand of hair round and round, a frightful thought enters my childish mind, "What if Mom should say I could not get married until I quit twisting my hair?!" So, bit by bit, I overcome that bad habit also.

Epilogue:

Thirty years later at a family reunion, after I was the mother of five children, I met an older cousin I'd been around as a child.

"Well, Annie," Katie exclaimed, "I see you're still *schtruwblich*!"

"Yep!" I replied, "I've been able to overcome many of my nervous childhood habits, but controlling my hair is not one of them!" And so, I've found out what people think. They think I'm *Schtruwblich*!

An Old Woman—Me?

"How do people get old and wrinkly?" I ask Mom as a shiver runs through me. I throw my arms across each other and hug them to my chest. "Will I get old too?" I think about some of the old people we visit who can't even walk or feed themselves. That would be awful!

"Yes," Mom says, "everyone gets old."

"I don't want to get old."

"Even baby Erla will get old," Mom says. I look at my little sister. She's so sweet and cute. How can she get old? I try to picture myself as an old woman, but it doesn't work. I have trouble seeing beyond the NOW! The BEYOND is a mystery to me.

Epilogue:

Now that I'm older, I've discovered what it's like! It's WONDERFUL! My children are grown, and even though I'm a widow, it's wonderful. There's no one telling me what to do, to go to bed or to get up. There's no one telling me that I'm lazy, to put my book down, or close my laptop and do something else (except my cat and my grandchildren).

It's WONDERFUL to look back and remember how God's loving hand has led me down the path of life. Yes, the LORD has been my shepherd, and life has been pleasant. I'm content to be classified among those who have trodden many foot paths in the course of their lives. But most of all, I'm thankful I'm not an insecure little girl anymore.

"Pitter-Patter"

"The days are too short," Mom says to herself, "too short to get everything done I need to do!"

It is late Saturday afternoon. The family's weekly supply of bread stands rising on the small table beside the cook stove. Just before it is ready to plop into the oven, my baby sister, Erla, comes pitter-pattering into the kitchen and pats down each loaf with her hands.

Milking time arrives. Mom sighs and looks at the rising loaves of bread. They are almost ready to bake again.

"Sarah," Mom calls, "pull up a chair and sit by the bread. Make sure the baby doesn't pat them down." Mom hustles to the basement, grabs the cleaned milk buckets and heads for the barn.

"When I return," Mom says to Daddy, "the bread will be ready to pop into the oven." But when Mom enters the kitchen after the milking is finished, she finds Sarah sitting by flattened lumps of dough. Silent tears are coursing down her checks. "Pitter-Patter Erla" is nowhere in sight.

"Didn't I tell you to watch that baby?!" Mom asks in a stern voice. Mom whips Sarah. It is getting late and the weekly supply of bread has not yet been baked.

"This time I'll watch the bread myself," Mom mutters, "there is no one else to trust." A long weary sigh escapes her lips as she moves the bread to a higher counter. Mom's not singing tonight as she usually does while she works in the kitchen. Soon a light evening meal is on the table. The bread is rising nicely and Mom's mind races ahead. "I'll soon place the loaves safely into the oven," she says as we are eating supper. Another deep sigh escapes her lips. "Then I'll bathe all of you and tuck you into bed while the bread is baking."

However, "Pitter-Patter Erla" slides a stool to the counter and pats the bread once more—and that, while Mom is guarding it!

Now it is very late. The family is asleep, but Mom is sitting beside the stove waiting to remove the baking loaves of bread. She feels bad. She, too, has failed to guard the bread from "Pitter-

Patter Erla" and has mercilessly whipped her eldest daughter for the same failing.

Epilogue:

Throughout the years Mother has often expressed sorrow over the incident of whipping Sarah for something in which she herself had also failed.

Too Many Decisions

"Annie! Get out from underneath my apron!" Mom briefly stops talking to the English stranger in front of her and pulls me out into the open. I drop my head, fold my arms, turn around and lean into her side. Gradually I creep back under the safety of the apron, but her strong arms pull me out again. I'm not bold like my brothers and sisters. When the folks go to town we usually stay on the farm. They need room to bring the supplies home, but on rare occasions like today we all go.

As I get older I get bolder and only duck under Mom's apron when someone speaks directly to me. I cannot understand English, but my brothers and sisters can.

"How about some ice cream?" Daddy asks after the shopping is done.

"Oh! Goody! Goody!" I jump up and down. We flock around Daddy and Mom like a bunch of chickens as we make our way down the hill to the ice cream parlor.

"Chocolate, strawberry or vanilla?" asks the man with the tall white hat behind the counter. He's looking straight at me. I can't make up my mind. I look at what the others have.

"Strawberry," I say. "Umm! Yumm! Yummy!" I lick my cone and follow Daddy down the street, but when I see the ice cream flavors the others have chosen, I feel dissatisfied.

"I wanted chocolate ice cream," I whine.

"Too late," Mom says, "you ordered strawberry!" I like strawberry, but I wonder what chocolate ice cream tastes like.

Sometimes Daddy orders milkshakes in tall frosty glasses, then we sit around little tables on the sidewalk and enjoy our cool treat. As usual, I eye the awesome colors and flavors the others have chosen, and am dissatisfied with mine.

"What does it taste like?" I ask Sarah. Hers is a soft green.

"If you want to know, get one yourself!" Sarah says.

"It's not fair," I say, "I didn't know they make them green!"

"Stop fussing, Annie," Mom says, "or we won't stop for ice cream again." I wipe my eyes and try not to look at what the others have, and then, I discover that mine is good too.

Always Hiding

"You go on," Mom says. "Hurry to the school bus. I'll hold Moses back a while so he won't hurt you." Our older brother hits and kicks us when the folks aren't around.

Our lane is a mile of curves and steep hills cut though the thick forest. Moses is tall and lanky while the rest of us have short Diener legs. I hear him coming a long way off. His bellows float through the air long before he appears around a curve in the lane behind us.

"Oh! Oh!" I whimper and scatter with the others to hide among the forest thickets. In my hidden spot I tremble as he quickly passes through. Fear grips my heart. It is hard to breath.

After his laugh fades off into the distance I wipe my eyes and scamper out of my hiding place and hurry along with the others toward the main highway. The bus has already passed and we have another mile to walk to school.

"You don't need to worry about Moses this morning," Mom says the next day as she hands each one of us a little round peanut butter tin with our lunch in it. "I've sent him on ahead to the bus stop."

We skip along merrily, chattering as we go. Suddenly, a piercing laugh erupts through the air. Moses jumps from the thickets on a high ledge along the forest edge and lands in our midst with his hands and legs thrashing in very direction.

"Ouch! Ouch!" We scream, scatter and escape into the forest while his laughter floats on down the lane toward the bus stop.

We tumble out of our hiding places and hurry on, but we've missed the bus again.

"I hate Moses!" I declare as I lift the corner of my apron and wipe away the dam of tears that are gushing out.

"You know you're not supposed to hate your brother," Sarah calls over her shoulder. I scurry to catch up with the others. At least I don't need to worry about Moses as we run the extra mile to school.

It seems as though we are always hiding from our brother. Hideous laughter, degrading language and pranks always announce his approach. Wherever I am, whatever I am doing, I scamper with the others to disappear. We hide in mangers, in hay mounds, under brooders, among the cows, in thickets, and behind rocks and furniture. But the best and safest place to hide is under Mom's apron. However, Mom is not always nearby.

When Moses is seventeen he runs away and joins the Air Force. It breaks Mom's heart. She stays in bed and weeps for days. We sisters corner Lester behind the kitchen door and make him promise not to run away and join the Air Force.

Then, Moses calls and informs Mom that he has changed his name to William. Again, Mom weeps, for he was named after her father, Moses. Now we call him Bill.

Epilogue:

Moses changing his name to William didn't change his character. However, his meanness changed into a more acceptable, yet uncouth, ornery disgust which remained unto the day of his death—which I now realize was an intimate relationship he reserved for his sisters only.

Glasses vs. Glasses

I enter the large dining room with a stack of water glasses and place one above each soup bowl on the table as Mom has taught me to do.

"I didn't do it!" my brother Moses shouts at Daddy.

"Then how did Betty's glasses get broken?" Daddy asks in a quiet voice.

"I guess they fell off her face and she stepped on them!" Moses' voice is very defiant. I stop what I'm doing and listen to the fuss going on at the other end of the dining room. What are they talking about? It makes no sense to me.

My parents have been informed that my brother Moses has broken a girl's glasses, and they are talking to him about it. Betty has said he knocked them off her face while she was sitting in the school bus, but Moses denies it.

"How do you put glasses on your face?" I ask as I set down the last drinking tumbler in its proper place.

"You hook them behind your ears," Mom replies.

"Dumb Annie!" my brother turns and snarls at me. I break into tears.

"How can a drinking glass make you see better? How can you fasten it behind your ears? I don't understand." Many questions tumble out of my mouth and a bucket of tears dims my eyes. No amount of explaining lifts the mystery. I lift the bottom of my dress and wipe my face.

"Dumb Annie!" Moses wiggles a finger under my nose. I burst another dam of tears. I ponder the mystery and ask gobs of questions all evening.

"Dumb Annie! You're so dumb!" Moses repeats.

"Your tears," Mom says, "could fill a washtub, and they don't help a bit." I go to bed with the others and sob myself to sleep.

The next day as I climb onto the school bus I scan for Betty. Toward the back of the bus I spot a girl with a big smile on her face. The nosepiece of her eyeglasses is taped together. Suddenly understanding comes to my dim, cloudy mind.

I Lie

"Annie!" Mom's stern voice calls from the open dining room door. "Annie, come here!" Slowly I climb up the steep bank of the small creek that runs along the edge of the backyard. It flows underneath the old weeping willow tree where we are playing and on behind the deep spring house where Mom keeps her milk, butter and cream cool. Then it meanders through the culvert under the lane, and runs along the other side of the road until it joins a larger creek at the edge of the forest.

"Hurry up!" Mom calls.

"Hurry up!" Mom calls the second time. "I don't have all day!" My feet are heavy as I slowly inch along until I stand gazing at her feet. Mom reaches down and tilts up my tear-stained face until I gaze into her eyes.

"Did you bite your sister?" she asks.

"No," I reply in a soft, almost inaudible voice as my eyes dart away from Mom's stern gaze.

"Oh yes, you did!" Lydie says calmly. She lifts up the bite mark on her arm. "See!"

"Who bit her if you didn't?" Mom asks.

"She bit herself," I sob. Mom looks at Lydie.

"Why would Lydie bite herself?"

"I don't know!"

"Did you bite her?" Mom asks as she tilts my face upward again. "I don't want people to think you weren't taught good manners."

"I didn't bite Lydie!" I say and burst into a full-fledged wail.

"Annie," Mom says sorrowfully, "you can't go to Heaven if you tell lies." I get a whipping that day, and the incident is forgotten except in the deep recesses of my memory.

An Understanding Squeeze

I wipe a few threatening tears away from my eyes, but what can I say? The facts have been spoken and I cannot refute them.

Uncle Obey and Aunt Obey Annie have come from our former home in Illinois to visit. It is chore time when they arrive.

"You children take good care of Uncle Obey and Obey Annie," Mom says as she goes down the cellar steps. "And Annie," Mom calls over her shoulder, "don't make a nuisance of yourself." A bit later I see her and the hired girl going around the outside of the house loaded down with the cleaned milkers and buckets.

Mom and the hired girl have scrubbed down the house from top to bottom. Of course, my sisters and I helped too. That's what you do when you know you are getting company.

Uncle Obey's have never seen our house, so while the folks are doing the chores we kids give a grand tour. I chatter with excitement as we gather around our guests. I stay snuggled close to Obey Annie. Mom says I'd been her special girl during the times Mom was sick before and after the twins were born.

"I love you, Obey Annie," I say, looking up into her kind face. She places an arm around my shoulder and gives me a special squeeze. A warm smile beams down at me and wiggles into my heart. I throw my arms around her waist and savor the sweetness of the moment.

Large, freshly made steel beds stand in each room upstairs.

"You don't want to come into this room!" my brother Lester announces as he blocks the doorway. "The girls sleep in here. It goes Pee! Pee! Pee! all night long." I burst into tears. Obey Annie puts an arm around my shoulder again and gives it an understanding squeeze as we move on into next room.

We Learn to "Make-Do"

The Depression is over, but then there is World War II. Many items that are needed for daily living are still scarce or rationed. Daddy needs government coupons to buy many things we need on the farm. Money is hard to come by, but Mom's an expert at supplying our needs.

Chicken and cow feed come bagged in cloth sacks. Mom patiently teaches us kids how to get hold of the right string and pull the seams open.

"Keep pulling," Mom says as she watches me. "Keep pulling until all the thread is free."

"I like it! It's fun!" I say as I pull and pull and pull.

"Here," Mom says. She takes the stick that's already bulging with string from my sister and hands it to me. "Wind your string on here," she says as she hustles on to the next one.

"This is fun too!" I exclaim as I wind and wind and wind.

Mom washes and bleaches the bags and then Sarah and Mom hang the snowy white squares on the long wash line that runs along the slope of the yard.

"Come on, Annie," Mom says, "hand me another bag." I like to see the many white squares of snowy white material flopping and dancing in the breeze.

"Annie!"

I hand Mom another bag.

On rainy days when Mom can't work outside she makes household linen on her treadle sewing machine. I stand on the other side and watch the needle's swift up-and-down motion as Mom treads the treadle and glides two bags together under the needle.

"It looks easy," I say.

"Stay back, Annie," Mom says. I've been edging closer and closer. "You're getting in my way!" Mom quickly sews four bags together to make a sheet or a tablecloth. She folds the feed bags in half to make pillow cases and cuts the bags in half for tea towels. Of course, she always hems everything.

"What are you doing?" I ask as I watch Mom spread an opened dyed bag on the table and pin homemade patterns made from newspaper onto it.

"I have to make Sarah a new dress. She's growing out of everything."

"I want a new dress too," I say.

"You have the dresses Sarah grows out of," Mom says, quietly. A pout creeps across my face.

"Annie," Mom says as she shoves me aside, "you're in the way." I back off a bit, but soon I'm back where the action is.

Mom presses all the surplus bags, folds them neatly, and stores them in Daddy's bottom desk drawer. People come to the farm to buy the cleaned, pressed squares of material from Mom.

The Dreaded Cure-all

Daddy is constructing a large new two-story chicken house on the slope above the garden. Workmen are swarming over the roof. My brothers, sisters and I are swarming around Mom in the kitchen.

"My stomach hurts," I wail. I compress my arms tightly around my waist and bend over.

"Me too," my sister groans. Mom pays little attention. She's busy whipping up a special dessert for Daddy and his workmen. I groan louder, flop myself on the floor, and roll back and forth. Soon the others are on the floor, rolling and groaning too. Our wails grow louder, but Mom ignores us.

When Mom reaches for the enema bag on top of the cupboard I know immediately I have made a bad mistake. A warm enema is Mom's "cure-all" for most of our ills.

I quit rolling as I watch Mom fill the bag with warm water.

"No! No! Mom!" I jump from the floor and clutch her arm, but Mom continues filling the bottle. I throw myself back onto the floor and wail.

"Come on," Mom says as she holds the side door open. I slowly get up off the floor and follow Mom and the others out the door and down the little path toward the new chicken house. When we reach the edge of the garden Mom turns left into the nearby pine grove.

"No! No!" I whimper and grab Mom's arm. "No! No! The men on the roof will see us!" By now there is a large chorus of protest rising from the pine grove.

"No," Mom says, "stop crying, the workmen won't see you. The trees are too thick, but if you keep on crying and making noise, they will hear you. Then what will they think?"

We all quiet down, but the pounding of the hammers and the pounding of my heart seem to be beating together as the jolly laughter of the workmen floats down among the pines. Slowly I lift my dress and drop the knee long-britches that Mom has made from bleached-out feedbags. They fall softly around my ankles. In spite of the thick pines, it is embarrassing, but before long I feel perky and happy again.

ERLA AND DADDY

April Fool

"Come on, girls," Mom says as she climbs out of the car and heads for the house. "We have company coming."

"Do they have a girl my age?" I ask Mom as I skip up the flat stone walk behind her. I don't stop to look at any of the fossil imprints, but follow Mom into the brick alcove and flop down on one of the loveseats between two tall stone pillars.

"Yes," Mom says as she stops in the doorway and turns towards me. "Come in and set the table!" But I linger. I want to see who is coming.

It is April the first! We've just arrived home from church. Daddy parked the black car in the wide stone-packed area between the barn and the hedge that runs along the edge of the yard. He and my younger brother, Lester, stand beside the car waiting. Instead of following Mom into the house, I turn and skip back down the stone path and join Daddy and my brother. They are gazing across the lane at the large vast flat field below us. It is the only flat area on our farm before the forest begins its ascent again toward Mount Davis, the highest peak in Pennsylvania.

"Look! There's a deer!" Lester exclaims. He points to the far corner of the field where a small creek maneuvers lazily along.

"Where? Where?" My eyes sweep swiftly across the field. "Where? I don't see a deer!"

"April Fool!" Lester announces triumphantly. He and Daddy laugh, but I feel like crying.

A black car drives in and parks beside Daddy's car. The mother and the older girls go into the house to help cook the meal. Daddy, the man and the boys head for the barn. A girl about my age lingers in the driveway by me. We climb the steep grade above the new henhouse. I jabber and giggle, but she's rather quiet.

"Look!" I say as I turn suddenly and point out across the lane to the field below us. "Look! There's a deer!" My friend searches for the deer just as I had done previously.

"I don't see a deer," she finally says.

"April Fool!" I say in a triumphant tone.

"Oh!" she exclaims. Horror sweeps across her face. "You told a lie! People who tell lies go to hell!"

"I didn't lie," I say. "It was a trick."

"No, you lied! There is no deer in the field! You will go to hell!"

"Dinner's ready," Mom's loud firm voice reaches us on the hillside. Two sober little girls sit squished on a tight long bench with the other children around the large dining room table that day. For me, the thrill of deceiving someone on April Fool's Day was destroyed forever.

Modern Times

It is hay-making time. Mom and we kids work in the fields right along with the men. A hay loader is dropping mounds of loose hay onto the back of the flat-bottom wagon. It's being pulled by Old Nancy and Sadie, our horses. We kids are stumping down the loose hay as the hired man moves it with a pitch fork to the front of the wagon. Mom and Daddy are following, one on each side of the wagon. They pick up loose bits that have been missed and toss them onto the wagon.

Mom's a hard worker. She's a tall, large, heavy woman; she's the oil that makes our home run smoothly and the glue that holds it together. Mom keeps up with the men when she works in the fields. Her heavy black stockings are rolled down to her ankles and her sleeves are pushed up above her elbows. Her hair is tightly pulled back into a thin bun. Mom has left her white pleated cap with thin long strings in the house along with her apron that has a long wrap-around belt that pins on one side. It's usually a different color then her dress and a bit shorter.

I try to pay attention to my job of stomping the hay, but it's hard with everything that is going on around me. I hear birds chirping in the nearby forest and the laughter of the tiny stream at its edge. I love to watch the birds and the beautiful clouds floating in the bright blue sky above me.

"Annie!" Mom calls in a sharp tone as she throws another pitch-fork full of hay up onto the wagon. "Stop your gawking and stomp that hay!" I give another little jump on a loose mound of hay. Why am I the only one Mom keeps probing on and on? "Annie, come on!" Mom calls again.

DADDY LATER USED HIS TRACTOR TO PULL THE HAY WAGON.

By late afternoon the last load of hay is gathered. I sigh and look at the big heavy team of horses. I bet they are glad too. Daddy stops the team at the rose arbor entrance to the house. We girls slide off the tall stack of hay into Daddy's arms then skip around Mom like playful pups as we follow her down the flagstone path that's full of fossils, around the house, and into the walk-in basement. Behind me I hear Daddy's gentle voice encouraging the horses as they slowly jostle the last load of hay up the steep hill toward the barn.

"I'm tired," Mom sighs as she loads our arms with milk buckets and strainers. "Oh!" she exclaims as she reaches up to a tall shelf above the window, "I almost forgot! We're out of fly spray in the barn." I love the barn and its smell, but tonight Mom's not the only one tired; I'm tired too. Long shadows are being cast in the yard from the many trees when we return to the house.

"Here," Mom says as she hands Lydie and I a large dishpan with a big round loaf of homemade bread in it. "Break this into chunks while I fetch the milk." Mom disappears out the back door. I hear the groan of the porch steps and the squeak of the spring house door. Soon she's back with a large pitcher of cool milk. She adds sugar to the chunks of bread and pours in the milk.

When Daddy comes up from the basement Mom carries the large heavy pan to the back yard. Sarah carries the tin bowls, while I carry the spoons.

The sun is starting to sink behind the horizon as I hold out my bowl for Mom to fill. I take my bowl and sit behind the long row of roses between the yard and the garden. Mom has told us how a little boy once sat by a rose arbor with his bowl of bread soup and a snake came and drank out of his bowl. The little boy hit the snake on its head with the back of his spoon. "*Nem awe brucka, nat ischt bree,*" he said. (Take some chunks, not just juice.) I hope a snake will come and sip out of my bowl too.

When the large dishpan is empty Mom rinses it, then fills it with clean cold water. We each rinse our bowls and spoons, then take them into the house and turn them upside down at our places at the table. The table now is set for breakfast.

"When I was a girl," Mom says, "we wiped out our bowls with a piece of bread, ate the bread, then turned our bowls over."

Mom scurries us up the stairs to bed. As I drop off to sleep I'm thankful that my breakfast bowl is rinsed and that I am living in modern times.

(THE ROSE ARBOR ENTRANCE TO OUR FARM IN PENNSYLVANIA.)

Back row: MOSES, SARAH HOLDING ERLA
Front row: TWINS – LESTER & LYDIE, ANNIE HOLDING LYDIE'S HAND

History Lessons

It is harvest time. Mom and we children work alongside the menfolks.

"I'm tired," Mom says late Saturday night as we come in from an exhausting day in the sun-baked harvest fields. "I'm too tired to bake and cook a big Sunday dinner for company tomorrow."

"We'll go to someone else's house instead," Daddy suggests.

"No," Mom says, "I just want to come home after church and sleep." But the custom, if you want company, is to prepare lots of food. If you don't, you drive to different farms until you find someone at home. So, especially during harvest time, many people gather at the same place.

I love these large gatherings. The women cook, exchange recipes, wash dishes and clean the kitchen while they chatter happily with each other. The teenage girls watch the babies and toddlers while the men and older teens inspect the barn and buildings. We children are free to play.

I especially like to visit the Tice Farm off Route 40 near Grantsville, Maryland. Their big old tall stone house is so big they don't use all the rooms. It used to be a hotel during the Revolutionary War. George Washington slept in one of the rooms upstairs whenever he came by this way. As I ramble with the other children through the rooms and listen to the adults talk, I get my first lessons on the Revolutionary War.

"You know," Daddy says to Mom, "it is harvest time. We'll probably get a house full of company if we come home."

"I'll fix a quick picnic basket and we'll go on a picnic. Then when we come home I'll take a nap." Mom says.

However, on this particular Sunday, before Mom's basket is packed a car drives in and my little brother Lester runs to the driveway to greet the company.

"*Meer hen nimmy nett can chooh vella*," (We never not any company wanted) he declares boldly. The folks come into the house laughing. Mom is embarrassed—she cares about what people think—so she quickly increases the picnic supplies, and then we head out the back lane for Mount Davis. Mom will at least get a quiet Sunday afternoon in the mountains.

After we've eaten our lunch we climb the tall steel observation tower. Round and round we go until we emerge on a large wooden platform with steel railings around the top. There is nothing on the entire structure to protect small children from falling to their deaths.

"Do not take the small children up the tower," Daddy had said to Mom. "It is too dangerous. I'll stay down here with them." But Mom takes us up anyway. Daddy is unhappy, and stays on the ground in quiet protest.

When we reach the top there is nothing to see but mile after mile of the scrub, gullies, rocks, and stunted pines that cover the mountain ranges. I feel as if I am on the top of the world looking down. I search until I find Daddy. He is standing beside our tiny black car looking up. His hands are on his hips. He's the size of the tiny tin soldiers I've seen in a store window.

HIGH POINT LOOKOUT TOWER
NEGRO MOUNTAIN, PA – 1953

When we begin our descent down the tower the openness of the stairwell frightens me. I begin to whimper. My distress becomes louder with each step down. Mom is carrying Erla. The twins are bravely forging ahead on their own, but not I. Then, suddenly, I am scooped up into my Daddy's strong arms and carried safely to the ground.

Epilogue:

I got my second lesson on the Revolutionary War when I was in Junior High. They loaded us on school buses and took us down

Route 40, past George Washington's Hotel. We traveled a long time before we came to Fort Necessity. It must have taken General Washington and his troops a long time to get there. That day the Revolutionary War stepped out of my history book and became a reality.

In sixth grade I had learned about the Civil War and the Underground Railroad. It had passed a mile from our village. Even though I was told that it was invisible, I looked for it, but I never found it. It became a great mystery! How could there have been a railroad you could not see?

I Try to Go to Heaven

It's a quiet calm evening as I quickly step into the pine grove. Peering back toward the direction from which I've come, I check to see if the others are in sight, then move deep into the grove until I find a spot of blue sky above the tall green tips. Expectantly, I lift my arms and heart toward Heaven. Nothing happens. Gazing into the serene, peaceful evening sky I lift my arms once more.

"Oh God," I say. "I want to come to live with you, too. Please make me go up like Jesus did!" Nothing happens. I ponder the mystery several minutes, then search for a larger patch of sky and lift my arms and heart toward Heaven the third time. Nothing happens. I hear the family coming so I retrace my steps and rejoin them.

Mom and we children work barefoot in the hot sun-baked stubbled harvest fields right alongside Daddy and the hired man. A stroll in the cool of the evening is a relaxing activity for our family after a quick supper of cold bread soup. Our favorite spot is the small clearing at the edge of the forest where, at sunset, deer come to graze. We call it the "Deer Patch." As we walk, we sing, and Mom and Daddy tell Bible stories. Sometimes we play Bible Popcorn—to see who can keep popping Bible verses the longest. We can't beat Mom and Daddy, they're good.

Tonight the story has been about Jesus raising his arms and ascending up into Heaven to live with God the Father. It seemed amazingly simple, but as usual, I peppered my parents with questions.

"What made Jesus go up?"

"Is Jesus still alive?"

"Can Jesus come back?"

"Can I go up too?"

And now, as I rejoin the group I flood my parents with more questions—questions they cannot answer.

"I raised my arms just like Jesus did. Why did I not go up?"

"Why did Jesus go up, and I didn't?"

"Doesn't God love me?"

"Why can't I go to Heaven too?"

"Well, Annie," Mom finally said in a sad low German voice, "you are not Jesus!"

Epilogue:

Sixty-odd years later I was resting on my couch when my adult kids came to inform me that the biopsy which had been taken was cancerous. I had a sudden flashback of the little Amish girl begging God to take her to Heaven. I jumped off the couch, began dancing around with my hands and face reaching upward. "NOW!"

"NOW!" I exclaimed. "NOW! Oh God, may I come to live with you in Heaven NOW?"

My son cleared his throat, "Now, wait a minute here!" he said.

"Mom, sit down!" his wife said. "You're being selfish! How do you think that makes us feel?" I fell with a plop onto the couch and in that moment, in one flash, all things whether great or small were brought into the embrace of God's Good, Perfect and Acceptable will. God's Grace became fresh and abundant, so that from surgery throughout radiation it has been one of the richest, most enjoyable experiences of my life.

Saturday Night

Mom has four girls and each girl has four braids. The Saturday night routine begins in the deep upstairs bathtub that stands on claw feet. In the high ceiling above is the hot water reservoir that fills from hot pipes crackling and creaking from the old coal furnace in the basement. Mom takes us out of the tub, scrubbed and clean according to our age (youngest to oldest) and dresses us in clean feed sack nightgowns. Then the braiding begins.

Baby Erla is first. Mom tosses a feed sack string across her head from ear to ear, and braids half of the string into the first front braid and hands it to Lydie to finish. Lydie is next. Mom hands me Lydie's braid with the long white string in it, and begins to divide my hair.

"Annie, hold still," Mom says as she snaps me on the head with the comb.

"Ouch!" I say, "How can I hold still when I'm braiding Lydie's hair?" I wipe my eyes with the back of my hand. Mom divides my hair in half from the tip of my nose up over the crown of my head and down the back. Then those halves are divided from ear to ear. Mom tosses a long white feed bag string across my head. I grab it.

"Annie, hold still." Mom slaps me with the comb again.

"Ouch," I cry and quickly drop the string. I wonder if this string is one I pulled out of a feed sack.

Mom braids the string into my front pigtail and hands it to Sarah to finish, then quickly braids Sarah's hair. She moves back to baby Erla and starts the process again until there are four braids on each of our heads. The front two braids are incorporated into the back two, string and all. Then Mom securely knots and pulls those braids into a tight bun at the back of each of our heads.

"Yippee!" I yell. My head feels tight and light. I skip down the stairs, through the dining room and out the side door. I shout at the top of my voice. I feel as if I am flying as I run through the yard.

In the morning Mom dresses us in our "Sunday best." She places black coverings over our heads, and we are ready for another service in the little Amish church nestled in the mountain coves.

Going to Church

"Annie, quit pulling out your hair!" Mom turns toward the back seat and slaps my fingers as she speaks. "Pull your apron down over your knees. You're wrinkling it!"

"Annie, hold still and be quiet!" Mom turns to speak to me again. It's Sunday morning and we've just pulled out of our mile-long lane onto the blacktop road. We're on our way to the (furthest away) church near Summit Mill.

"Annie, stop picking your nose! Take your finger out of your mouth! What will people think? They'll think I didn't teach you anything!" I am the only one in the back seat who needs constant supervision. The others know what is expected of them, but not me.

"Annie, stop chewing your cap strings! Take them out of your mouth!"

"Annie, be quiet!"

"Annie, hold still!"

"Annie, stop crying!"

Daddy turns off on the Compton Mill Road, but we call it "*Kutz Vake*" because it tosses us as it twists and turns though the low valleys and high ridges. We get sick to our stomach.

"I'm going to *kutz* (throw up)," someone says with an urgent wail. Daddy slams down on the brake and the car comes to a sudden stop. Mom tumbles out and hurriedly pulls us out of the back seat. She lines us up along the ditch. Mom pulls a handkerchief out of her pocket and wraps it around her finger, then "spitz" on it.

"No!" I cry and sink away. "I don't want a *spitz* bath." Mom grabs my arm and pulls me closer. I close my eyes as I feel the moist hankie firmly wiping the edges of my mouth.

"Hold still, Annie!" Mom says sharply. She cleans me, then pushes me into the car and grabs my brother. She's in a hurry. She doesn't like being late for church. When we're all in the car, Daddy takes off with a jerk.

"If you think my *spitz* baths are bad," Mom says as she turns toward the back seat, "you should have seen the *spitz* baths my mother gave Johnny and me. I despised being cleaned in the buggy with a wet finger. We lived in Kansas. It was hot and dusty. At least I wrap my finger into a handkerchief first."

"Annie, stop picking your nose!" Mom slaps my finger and then turns back to the front.

"I have to go bathroom," I say urgently as I hop to my feet and squeeze my legs together. Poor Mom is frazzled by the time Daddy pulls the car up to the long tall porch that runs the length of the church. He climbs out and lifts us, one by one, onto the tall porch.

The children meet in the women's cloak room for Sunday School. Several ladies teach us the German ABC's. We sing choruses and learn verses. Then one of the ladies tells us a Bible story.

After Sunday School we file into the main room where a big old pot-bellied stove stands in the center. The old folks sit around it—The men and boys on one side of the room, and the women and girls on the other. The backless benches are high. I swing my legs as we sing slow German songs. My favorite is "*Gott Ist De Liebe*" (God Is Love). The leader sings out the first phrase of each line and then the congregation joins in. It takes a long time to sing one song.

My baby sister is having trouble holding still today. She shifts and lifts her dress higher and higher. She wants everyone to see her first pair of "bought" panties. I've never had "bought" panties. I wonder what it would feel like to wear something so soft. Mom makes mine out of bleached feedbags. They're rough and stiff, but after they've been washed several times they begin to soften.

We listen to three preachers, but my mind keeps going back to my baby sister and her "bought" panties. Finally, I fall asleep. I'm happy when I awake, because now I don't have to take a nap when we get home, but that only works when Mom doesn't want to take a nap. She says she can't sleep with us running around making noise.

After church I search out the old Grandmas and Grandpas. They always have some "goodies" in a little bag or tied up in a handkerchief for us children. I know which ones have the best treats. When Daddy pulls the car up to the long tall porch he lifts us back into the car and we head home, unless the folks have been invited out or they decide to visit at someone else's house.

Neighbors!

We have three neighbors. Henry Yoders' live at the entrance of our mile-long lane on the hard-topped road. We go to the same church, and they have children our age. I like going to their farm for Sunday dinner.

Enos Benders lives a mile down the other direction of our lane. He often stops and picks us up in his buggy. His wife is sickly. We enjoy carrying notes and little tidbits from our Mom to her. Their walls are covered with old calendars. I like to look at the pictures, but I don't stay long because they don't have any girls. They only have two boys. I don't like playing with boys, they're bossy.

The Baker family lives miles away if you go out our long lane, up the mountain road toward Mount Davis, then down their long lane. Even so, our farms back up to each other. We have a foot trail worn along the fields and through the woods. They have a large family of boys, with a few girls our age. Our moms have an agreement that we cannot visit each other until a return visit is made.

"Mom! Mom!" my sisters and I bounce up and down in front of her. She's shelling peas. "Can we go play with the Baker girls?"

"Whose turn is it?" Mom asks.

"Ours," my sisters and I say in unison.

"After all the peas are shelled," Mom says as she keeps popping the tiny green emeralds from their shells. I reach into Mom's pan and grab a handful of peas and let them roll slowly through my fingers.

"Get out of my pan," Mom says. "Get your own!" The cupboard rattles as I dig for a proper container. Shelling peas takes forever, especially if there's something else I want to do. It is mid-afternoon before we joyfully skip down the lanes and over the mountain fields to our friends' house.

Milking Time

"Le-s-s—ter! Ly-d-d-ie! An-n-n—ie!" Mom's clear high-pitched voice floats among the trees in the old apple grove where the twins and I are playing. We drop what we are doing, crawl under the barbed wire field fence, hop across the small creek, and head for the high porch at the back of the tall brick house.

"Time to fetch the cows," Mom says as she meets us at the back door with a plate of cookies, a tin cup, and a pitcher of cool milk. She's fetched the milk up from the deep springhouse. I take my turn drinking from the cup and grab a large church cookie for each hand. We call them Obey Annie Church Cookies, because

Mom got the recipe from Aunt Obey Annie while we lived in Illinois.

I skip happily with the others up the path past Daddy's new henhouse. We turn left and follow the stone-strewn lane that leads to the mountain-side pasture. Lester grabs the narrow fence pole of the gate, which is two lines of barbed wire stretched across the opening, and walks it backward along the fence. Inside the gate we turn right and head for the "Hill." A lot of our play time is centered on the "Hill."

"Wait for me," I call to the twins, who are forging ahead. I'm out of breath, my side aches, and my leg muscles are tight and twitching. But in their excitement to reach the top, the twins pay no attention. By the time I join them they're ready to move on, but not me. I'm exultant! I swing out my arms and twirl. I feel as if I'm standing on top of the world. I sing. I shout. I laugh. I can see for miles and miles. I see pieces of the little village of Springs and the highway as it winds its way toward Salisbury. There are little farms nestled here and there. Our boundary fence line runs across the top of the "Hill," and some cow paths approach from several directions. Even though there's not much for a cow to eat up here, we often find one or two strays.

Today there are no cows, so I hustle after the twins toward the maple syrup camp. It's in the lower ground in the midst of the maple grove. That's where we usually find the cows lying around in the luscious grass, taking life easy. The lead cow automatically gets up and slowly heads down the trail toward home. The others straggle along behind.

When the cows reach the barnyard, Daddy opens the barn door and each cow files into her stall.

"Clank!"

"Clank!"

"Clank!" go the stanchions as Daddy closes each cow's head into its proper place. The grain troughs are already full and the cows chew contentedly. Their tails swish at the pesky flies. Daddy brushes and sprays the cows before he washes each udder, then strips a squirt of milk out of each teat before putting on the suction cups of the milker. The barn cats follow Daddy down the row of cows. Each is anxiously waiting its turn for the squirt of milk to land in its mouth.

The tall cans of milk are hauled to the milk house, where they stand in cool water awaiting the arrival of the milk truck in the morning.

In the summer the cows are turned out into the barnyard lot for the night, but during the winter Daddy keeps them in their stalls. After milking, he beds the cows down with fresh straw.

"Come," Daddy says on cold winter nights, "let's pitch the straw down." We follow him through the darkening barn, past the horse stable, and up the old rickety steps. I think of Daddy's horses, which he sold, as the old steps squeak under my feet. I like throwing loose straw down from the upper barn loft through the hole in the floor. It's centered between the two rows of cows. When the pile is big enough Daddy jumps down, turns, and stretches his arms upward.

"Oh, goodie, goodie!" I exclaim. I can hardly wait until it's my turn to jump into his strong arms.

Epilogue:

One night Daddy dreamed I was about to jump out of the hay loft without a pile of hay below. In his sleep he ran to my room and caught me as I fell out of bed!

Unpleasant Duties

Uncontrollable sobs cause me to shake and stumble as I slowly make my way toward the barn. Darkness has settled over the farm nestled in a little valley high in the Allegheny Mountains. The strong winter winds tear at the wraps around my slim body and threaten to blow out the lantern I am carrying. Warm milk splashes from the heavy bucket that bangs against my leg.

I set the lantern and bucket on the ground and struggle to slide back the heavy barn door and slip through the narrow opening. The two German Shepherd pups Uncle Dan gave us scamper around me, whimpering and wiggling their welcome. They are of little comfort as I shiver, cry and stumble on.

A warm moist feeling accompanied by the sour-sweet smell of the silage prevails. My eyes follow the large stone wall that runs the length of the barn. Every crack and crevice is filled with dirt, dusty webs and bits of straw. Upon it rests the weight of the hay lofts above. Small dusty windows filled with cobwebs and bits of trash are set high in the stone wall. They almost touch the ceiling. Beneath, along the wall a few odd pieces of unused equipment are half-hidden in mounds of old dusty hay.

I hear the rough lick of a tongue as a cow retrieves the last kernels of her grain. A stanchion rattles as another cow flops onto her freshly bedded slab. A bat darts in front of my face. I duck. Another drench of tears flows freely down my cheeks.

The lantern casts eerie shadows, distorting the features of the barn. Strange, frightening sounds surround me as the animals shift here and there. The calf pen, to which I am headed, is down a narrow hallway in the middle of the barn. The large heads of the work horses nod in the lantern light as I slip by.

Tonight, darkness has fallen before Daddy has finished separating the milk in the walk-in basement of our large four-story brick house. The others have taken their turn in carrying the warm skimmed milk back to the calves. I am last. Complete darkness has fallen and a strong wind has risen.

"Please Daddy? Please? Please?" I beg. I weep. "Please, don't make me go alone in the windy black darkness!"

"The others have taken their turn. They didn't cry. Go, feed the last calf!" And so, I am slowly plodding through the dark barn toward the calf stall with a bucket of warm skimmed milk.

When I come to the pen I set down the lantern, then lift the heavy bucket over its wooden side and hook it on the inside of the top rail. A barn cat quietly drops from the nearby stairway onto the railing near me. Only one calf comes to claim its meal. The others are curled up, sleeping. I wonder if this last calf has been crying like me. With a thrust against the bucket the noisy slurping and sucking begins. I hear the swish of the tail as it beats against one side of the calf and then the other. I wipe away a few more tears.

With a push and a shove the calf empties the bucket. I struggle to unhook it from the railing. I don't look behind me as I slip out of the barn and slide the heavy door closed. The empty bucket and the lantern bounce against my legs as I run toward the safety of the house.

Little Brother's In Control

Daddy is not farming with horses anymore. He has sold them and bought an Allis-Chalmers tractor, but he misses his horses.

"A man can never forget a good team of horses like Old Nancy and Sadie," Daddy often says. He had brought them along from the Illinois farm.

The new tractor doesn't acknowledge Daddy's presence like the horses had, nor does it get excited when Daddy fills its tank with gas. So, frequently on Sunday afternoons we stop to visit the horses on the way home from church. He calls and they answer. Soon they come racing, with their tails flying high, around the corner of the old wooden barn at the edge of little dusty country road. I crawl out of the car and stand beside Daddy. Timidly, I reach up and stroke one of the big noses. Daddy leaps across the rail fence.

"Remember," Mom calls from the car, "you have your Sunday suit on." Daddy ignores Mom and throws his arms around Old Sadie's and Nancy's necks. They quietly neigh and nudge his pockets, but Daddy doesn't have a treat for them in his "Sunday best" suit. Daddy is very quiet as we drive on home.

Daddy likes his new tractor, too, though. It works his fields much faster and is not as time consuming to maintain.

One hot summer day while Daddy is cultivating the large corn field across the lane from the house he leaves the tractor idling at the edge of the field while he climbs across the ditch to get a cool drink of water from the deep springhouse. Mom comes out of the house to talk with Daddy. Suddenly, they hear the tractor kick into gear. They twirl around to see my little brother Lester driving the tractor down a long row of corn toward the small creek that runs between the field and the forest.

Mom and Daddy yell, hop across the ditch, then scurry across the fence while the hired man comes running out of the barn. They wave their arms and yell. The hired man with his long legs catches up with the "Little Run-Away" just as he comes to the end of the row. Lester reaches down and turns off the tractor.

"How did you know how to stop the tractor?" the hired man asks.

"Well, dumb!" Lester says as he slides down off the seat. "How do you stop a tractor?" The hired man continues to cultivate while Mom, Daddy and Lester return to the house. They retrace the path of the tractor. Not one stalk of corn has been uprooted!

Rotten Eggs

"Hey, look what I found!" I exclaim, holding up several eggs for the twins to see. "I'm going to hatch them!"

"Dumb!" Lester says, "People don't hatch eggs!"

"Well, I'm going to. I'm going to have my own chickens."

"Dumb!"

"They're probably rotten," Lydie says as she tilts her chin slightly.

"No, they're not!" I bristle a reply. Fast running footsteps pound the ground outside the barn. The color drains out of my face. Fright seizes my heart like icy fingers.

"It's Moses," I whimper. "Where can we hide?" My eyes dart around the empty unused stable. Lester and Lydie tumble into the hay manger where I'm standing. We sink deep into its shadows.

Since Daddy sold the work horses the stable has been our favorite place to play. I hold still and stare at the two small dusty web-filled windows that almost touch the ceiling on the outside wall. A curdling cry rips through the air. It sends chilly shivers up and down my spine. Gradually the footsteps fade away.

"I hate Moses," I whimper.

"Mom says we must not hate our brother," Lydie says.

"But, he's going to kill me," I quiver.

"Nnaw," Lester says, "not as long as I'm around." He crawls out of the manger onto the narrow wooden steps in the hallway that lead to the hayloft above.

"Don't count your chickens before they're hatched," Lydie says over her shoulder as she scampers after him.

What does she mean? I have seven eggs. Isn't that the same as seven chickens? I wonder how many meals I will miss? How many nights I'll sleep in the barn? I move my nest deeper into the manger.

Another sharp cry rips thought the air. The barn door squeaks and rolls back on its track followed by a hideous laugh. I hear Moses' lanky arms and legs thrashing about. A puppy yelps. I can't move. A large lump fills my throat. My mouth is dry. I feel tipsy. I jump as hay falls into the manger from the opening in the hayloft above. With a soft crush it completely covers me.

"The twins." I murmur. "How do they always know what to do?"

Seconds later, Moses rips open the hallway door and gives the side of the manger a deafening blow with the broad side of his boot as he lets loose another blood-curdling scream. I squeeze my eyes shut and hold my breath. A shiver runs down my back. Dots dance before my eyes. Moses leaps up the rickety steps two at a time.

"All you dumb kids come to the house for dinner," he yells as he runs out of the hayloft door, down the barn bank, and on toward the house. I take a deep breath. My right leg is tingling. I rub it, shift my weight, then count my eggs.

"Good," I say, "at least my eggs are OK." In the distance I hear the house door slam.

"Annie," Mom's shrill, stern voice brings tears to my eyes. With a quick stroke I wipe them away. The stable door opens with a jerk.

"The dumb thing's in here," Moses says, pulling back the hay. I am petrified. Mom is standing with her stout arms propped on her heavy hips behind him. Mom reaches into the manger and with one easy stroke pulls me out.

"That dumb thing is trying to hatch rotten eggs!" Moses says. "Dumb!" He pokes a crooked finger into my face. I burst into tears.

"You cannot hatch eggs like a hen," Mom says.

"Dumb!" Moses shakes another finger at me. He reaches into the manger and delivers the eggs three at a time into Mom's uplifted apron.

"No! No!" I scream and jump up and down as I claw at Mom's arms. "I want my eggs! I want to hatch them!"

"Hee! Hee! Hee!" Moses laughs as he shakes a crooked finger under my nose.

"Annie," Mom scolds, "these eggs are rotten! They will not hatch!"

"No! No!" I scream. I'm still jumping up and down in front of Mom. She's tall and stout. "Don't break my eggs! I found them! They're mine!"

"Hee! Hee! Hee!" Moses laughs.

It's a solemn assembly that moves with Mom out to the large rock pile beside the barn. Torrents of tears stream down my face. Moses reaches into Mom's apron and throws a handful of eggs against the rocks. A horrible stink erupts into the air. I collapse to the ground.

"Look for yourself, Annie," Mom says as she lifts and guides me toward the sticky, stinky, gooey mess on the large rocks. She wipes my face with her apron and pushes me closer. I pinch my fingers over my nose.

"Dumb Annie!" Moses yells with each handful he throws. I turn and run with the others to the house while my well-made plans are being crushed against the rocks.

Epilogue—1977:

All twenty-seven of us were gathered for a professional family portrait. Grandparents, aunts, uncles, cousins and in-laws stood in ready anticipation. Suddenly, just before the click of the shutter a handful of eggs reached out.

"Annie," my oldest brother said, "I thought you would smile better if you had some eggs to hatch! These aren't rotten, either!"

Then, "Click!" went the shutter of the camera, and my egg story was forever preserved in a family portrait!

Back Row: **Lester Diener** with wife **Marlene Diener, Carol** (Shafer) **Diener** - wife of **Bill** (William) **Diener** holding eggs, **Sheri Walter** daughter of **Gordy Walter & Erla** (Diener) **Walter** oldest daughter **Tami Walter, Sally** (Sarah Diener) **Brown.**

Middle Row: Son **Rex** & daughter **Laresa** of Lester Diener, Son **Greg** of **Al Miller & Lydie** (Diener) **Miller, Anna** (Annie Diener) **Yoder** - mother of **Eugene Yoder**, wife of **Arnold Yoder** who is holding youngest son, **John Yoder.**

Third Row: **Niel & Ritch Diener** sons of Lester Diener, **Connie Miller** daughter of Lydie (Diener) Miller, Diener Mother and Grandmother **Barbara** (Mast) **Diener, Hugh & Todd Yoder** sons of Anna (Annie Diener) Yoder.

Front Row: **Joanne Miller** daughter of Lydie (Diener) Miller; **Barbara, Andrew** & **Mary Yoder**, daughters & son of Anna (Annie Diener) Yoder

Comfort of Cats

"Annie! Lydie!" Mom calls. "Go up to the hen house and stuff fresh straw into the nest boxes. The straw is already there. Don't miss any boxes." We merrily skip up the path to Daddy's new two-story hen house. As we open the door to the bottom floor we are greeted with a fresh heap of straw. We happily stuff straw into the boxes on the lower floor, then load our arms with straw and move to the upper floor. We make several trips down the stairs for more straw.

"Oh!" I exclaim and run to the window facing the house when I hear the dining room screen door slam. "It's Moses! He's coming this way!" Fear grips my chest. I run in circles, looking for a place to hide. Then I see Lydie calmly sliding through the small opening at the top of the large round hood of the chick brooder that is being stored in the entryway at the top of the stairs. I slide in after her and roll to the dark primmer of the low hood. Moses' feet come pounding up the stairs.

"Where are you dumb girls?" Moses yells and lets loose a hideous laugh as he gives the brooder top a vicious kick. My heart beats loudly in my chest. "Mom wants you dumb girls in the house!" Soon he's gone. I hear the outside door slam. I lay still a few minutes longer. Slowly, my eyes adjust to the dimness.

"Look!" Lydie exclaims. "Here are baby kittens!" All thoughts of returning to the house vanish as we engage ourselves in the wonder of a fresh litter of kittens. As we lay quietly cuddling our new-found treasures we drop off to sleep. When I awake Lydie is climbing out of the hood. I follow. We leave our secret hidden under the hood and scurry to return to the house. However, the entrance door is locked from the outside. I hear Moses' feet pounding the dirt path again.

Lydie turns and scrambles up the stairs. I follow. She crawls under the chickens' roosting racks, yanks out the small wooden manure door, and drops onto the pile of manure below. I wonder how she always knows what to do. By now, Moses' footsteps are pounding up the stairs. I am frightened as I look down on the huge manure pile. Lydie scampers to her feet and runs to the house. I close my eyes and drop through the hole. I hit the top of the pile and roll to the bottom.

"Ha! Ha! Ha!" I hear Moses roar as I unscramble to my feet and follow my sister to the house. "My dumb sisters think it's fun to roll around on a pile of manure!"

Sherman Davis

My folks bought the farm at the foot of Mount Davis from an old gentleman named Sherman Davis. He and several generations before him were raised on this historic spot. In fact, the first Davis was a surveyor for the state of Pennsylvania, and the Governor of Pennsylvania gave him the whole mountain and named it "Mount Davis" after him.

Sherman has many stories to tell us. He and his wife have moved to the little village of Springs. My Mom named our baby sister after Sherman's sister, Erla.

"If you're going through Springs," I hear Mom call down the stairs to Daddy as he comes into the basement, "I'd like to go along and visit with Sherman's wife."

"Can we go? Can we go?" we children come rumbling from throughout the house and surround Mom. I bounce up and down and grab her apron.

"Oh! Goodie!" I yell when Mom gives me a positive nod. I can hardly wait. We love to cluster around Sherman's big old rocker and listen to his stories and words of wisdom while Mom visits with his wife.

I love the stories about his childhood when he lived at the very same place we are living now. He tells us how it used to be before the big brick house was built and how his father built the two-story springhouse over the spring that's been bubbling up out of the ground even before the beginning of recorded time. He tells us how every generation of teenage of boys has gotten thrills by walking the dangerous steel railing on top of the Mount Davis Tower.

"It's hundreds of feet in the air," he says. "It sits on the highest point in the Allegheny Mountains of Pennsylvania." He sighs and is silent. A far-away look comes into his eyes.

"You must never do that," he finally says. "It was foolish and very dangerous for us boys to do that."

"I was a government survivor, just like my daddy and granddaddy before me," he says, changing the subject. "That job was full of adventure and danger too." He reaches over to a small table beside his chair and picks up a box.

"Let me show you my collection of special specimens and rocks I've found throughout the years." Every object he picks up for us to examine has an interesting story.

"I found this one when I was a boy." He picks up a stone with a snake imprint in it. "I found many of these while I was splitting rock on your farm. If you'll look closely at the rocks that form the sidewalk going from the rose arbor to the front alcove of the house, you'll find more fossil imprints. These all came from the slopes of your farm."

"This flower," he picks up another stone and runs his finger tenderly over the tiny imprint, "only grows along the sea coasts in warm southern climates, but I found it in the Rockies. This proves that there was a worldwide flood! But," he interjects, "you are too young to understand about that." We grin at each other. We don't think we are too young.

"Children," Mom says, "it's time to go."

"I don't want to go," I say. "I want to hear more stories."

"I'll show you more of my collection the next time you come," Sherman says as Mom herds us out the door. I think about Sherman's stories for many days before they begin to fade away.

Sherman and his wife live across the dirt road from the village school.

"Please, Mom," I beg when I'm a bit older and speaking English. "Please write a note to the teacher so she will let me visit Sherman during dinner recess." So, once a week, I happily skip across the ditch and road and knock on Sherman's door. These are the shortest noon hours of the week.

Epilogue

After my family moved to Springs, I got to visit Sherman frequently. About the time I entered Junior High in Salisbury, Sherman and his wife moved to the same town, and I continued my frequent noon visits. I never tired of Sherman's stories and scientific explanations. I introduced him, his collections, and his wisdom to our science class when I was in high school. My classmates loved him. He's a bit feeble now, but his mind is still sharp.

"I can't tell you about this precious stone," Sherman says one day as he fondly holds a tiny jeweled stone in the tips of his long fingers. He examines it carefully. "You are too young to understand the marvels of God's creation." That day I realize that my friend Sherman is beginning to fade away. I am sad. He soon passes on, and my family moves to Nappanee, Indiana, but I've never forgotten my friend Sherman Davis and our common linkage—the old Sam Davis farm with its exotic large four-story brick and stone house.

HIGH POINT

Sherman's First Story

"I was adopted," Sherman Davis says. He looks at the cluster of us children gathered around his chair.

"When I was a boy we lived in a little clapboard house on your farm. The big brick house with the stone alcove porch that you live in wasn't built then." My eyes grow big with wonder.

"My mother wasn't very well, so she always had a hired girl to help her. As I got older the hired girls didn't like me. Of course, if I wouldn't have teased and played pranks on them, things might have been different. I was a pretty good-sized boy already when one hired girl picked me up and ran to the horse's water tough outside the barn. She held my head under the water. She did this every time I made her mad. I'd tell my folks, but they believed the hired girl instead of me.

"When I was a bit older I decided to get even with her. I knew she loved apples, so I went to the orchard and found a big red juicy apple. I carved out the inside and made it hollow, then I stuffed it with gritty dirt, bugs, manure, and worms.

"'Give me that apple!' the hired girl said when she saw me holding it.

"'No,' I said, 'I found it! It's mine!'

"'Give it to me!'—she tried to snatch it out of my hand.

"'OK,' I finally said. 'You can have one bite, but, I'm going to hold it.' She grabbed my wrist and took a great big old bite. She sputtered, coughed, and turned red. Boy, was she mad! I laughed and laughed, but I should have cleared out of there. She grabbed me and dragged me to the water tough and shoved me under. She would have drowned me if my father hadn't come into the barnyard and caught her. He was furious. My father fired her. After I was OK again, I got a good licking for tormenting the hired girl. That day I learned to be kind to everyone, and I hope you children will also be kind. In life there will be people who don't treat you right, but you children should always be kind in return."

Sherman's Second Story

Sherman Davis begins all his stories alike, "When I was a boy..." We sit eagerly around his knees waiting to hear another adventure from days gone by. "When I was a boy," he repeats, "your farm had a lot of good maple trees. There were sugar trails running in and out among the clusters. It was my job to help lug those big buckets of sap to the waiting tank. It was mounted on mud skis and pulled by a heavy team of work horses.

"One early spring day my dad sent me to see how the sap was running. I went down the lane toward the main road. The lane ran along the long flat field which lay across from the house and barn before it began its ascent up and down and around the hollows and large rocks toward the road. A row of maple trees grew on the edge of the forest at the far end of the field. I checked the hanging buckets and then climbed to the top of my favorite tree. I was perched among the bare branches when a fancy city buggy from Pittsburgh came around the curve in the lane. It stopped at the edge of the field." Sherman chuckles.

"'Hey,' the man called up to me. 'Is this where I can buy some fresh maple syrup?'

"'Yes,' I answered. 'Drive on up to the house.'

"'What are you doing up in the tree?' the man asked. He seemed puzzled.

"'I'm squeezing the sap out of the branches! See how it is dripping into the bucket? When the bucket is full we cook it until it turns into syrup.' The man asked several more questions then drove on toward the house. I slipped down from the tree and climbed up another. When the city slicker drove back out the lane, we waved to each other. After he was out of sight I jumped out of the tree and ran to the house. I wanted to share the prank I'd played on the man.

"My father met me at the door with a razor strap in his hands. 'What kind of tales have you been telling, Sherman?' he asked. My father wasn't very happy with the description the visitor had given of our maple-sugaring process. I learned that day not to have fun on someone else's ignorance. If you children are wise you also will be careful not to have fun at someone else's expense."

Sherman's Third Story

"When I was a boy," Sherman begins. I nestle closer to his chair and look up eagerly into his face. He smiles down at me. "Neighborhood people would get together and help each other with big projects. I remember hearing about some neighbors that had gotten together to butcher their fall hogs. They lived further up the mountain range toward Mount Davis than we did. Night began to fall before they were completely done. The visiting family hurriedly wrapped their portion of the pork into newspapers, loaded their wagon and began their journey home. It was very cold, and the sun had dropped behind the mountains, so they had wrapped their infant baby in newspapers also. They journeyed down the mountainside with their faithful farm dogs following.

"The progress was rough and slow. They heard a pack of wolves howling in the distance. They hurried their team along, but the wolves were gaining. The dogs bristled and growled. They threw out a pack of meat to the wolves. After it was devoured the wolves were on their trail again. After losing several packages of meat, the family finally reached their home safely. Then they discovered that the baby had been thrown to the wolves!

"The father and teenage sons mounted horses and rushed back up the mountain trail. They found the baby surrounded by wolves with their faithful farm dogs standing guard over it.

"There was a lot of rejoicing in that home that night, don't you think?" Sherman asked as he looked into our uplifted faces. "It was not only the dogs that protected that baby, but God Almighty himself sent the child's guardian angel to ward off the hungry wolves!"

Sherman's Fourth Story

"When I was a boy," Sherman starts another story. I nestle in closer to his chair. "We didn't have fencing for our cattle like we do today. In the spring we would brand our livestock and turn them loose onto the mountainside. The mountain ranges were steep and rocky with many deep crevices too wide to leap across. There wasn't much grass, and the cattle wandered far and wide looking for food. Of course, we kept our milk cows and farm horses close by. Then in the fall, before the heavy snows set in, we had to search across the ranges to find our cattle. If a neighbor ran across someone else's cattle, they would send word as to where the cattle had been seen.

"One fall a young boy begged to go with his father to bring in their cattle. The lad was young and he slowed down the process for his father. The boy became hungry and cold. Soon he was whining and crying. The father became very impatient and upset. He scolded the lad harshly. Finally, in a fit of anger, he threw his son down a deep crevice and went on without him." I gasp, then breathe heavily. Sherman places a hand on my head.

"The man found his cattle," Sherman says as he looks down at me, "and brought them home. He told his family the boy had wandered off and he could not find him. The neighbors helped search the mountain ranges, but the boy was not found.

"The father became very irritable and impossible to live with. His mind finally collapsed and he had to be put into a mental institution. On his deathbed he confessed what he had done to his son, but then it was too late to make any restitution.

"Children," Sherman says as he looks at the solemn faces around him, "when you do wrong, confess it right away. Don't let anger or any other sin destroy your life" I sit transfixed and quiet for several minutes. Then I get up with the others and scamper home. (Of course, we are living in Springs by now.)

Supper Time

"Come on, girls," Mom says. She's standing barefoot in front of the large cast-iron stove. It is standing in an outside corner of the large kitchen. Mom's sleeves are rolled up above her elbows. She's singing a soft German tune as she stirs the bubbling tomato gravy and keeps an eye on the heating hominy. She wipes her hands on her apron, throws her covering strings back over her shoulders, and turns from the stove.

Mom's kitchen is very handy with its crude plumbing that flows down from the large hot water reservoir strapped to the ceiling in the upstairs bathroom. In the winter, when the furnace in the basement is used, the water circulates through it and stays hot. In the summer, Mom keeps a teakettle full of water on the cast-iron stove. It heats while she cooks our meals. Mom carries the dirty water out the back door and throws it off the high porch into the bushes below.

"Come on, girls," Mom says again. "Finish setting the table!" My sister Lydie is placing the water tumblers at each bowl. I have a handfull of spoons. Sarah is struggling with a large loaf of homemade bread. She's trying to cut the slices thick and even, just the way Mom likes them when we have tomato gravy to dip over them. Mom prides herself on the neat nutritious meals she places on her table three times a day.

"Annie!" Mom says as she enters the dining room with the steaming bowl of tomato gravy. (She never places her cookware on the table.) "Annie! Pick up all the spoons and lay them down right! You can do better than that!" I wipe away a few silent tears. Why is Mom never pleased with my work? Why doesn't she scold Lydie and Sarah?

"Dumb!" Moses pokes a crooked finger into my face. I burst into tears. Sarah smuggles a paper bag under the table. She places her legs into it. Her legs are black and blue because Moses kicks her under the table. Today when he kicks we hear the bag rattle. He doesn't do it again.

"I don't like gravy tomatoes," Moses says.

"Sit up and eat!" Daddy says. "You can't leave the table until your plate is clean." But at bed time Moses' plate still isn't clean.

God's Care

"Daddy! Daddy!" the twins, Sarah and I screech. I jump to my feet in the back seat of the car with the others and pound the seat in front of me. My older brother Moses has remained on the farm with the hired man to help with the chores.

"Sit down, hold still and be quiet!" Mom commands from the front seat. She's clutching little Erla into her bosom. Obediently, we sink into the back seat and watch in horror as the car slides back and forth. An occasional cry of terror escapes our lips and we are on our feet again, pounding the backs of our parents.

We are returning home from Illinois. Grandpa Diener has been very sick. Dusk is gathering. We're in the middle of an ice storm on Route 40 approaching a steep slope near Wheeling,West Virginia. When we reach the top the pavement changes before it begins its long, straight decent. Suddenly, the car swerves as it hits the ice-covered bricks. Instantly, we are on our feet screaming and pounding Daddy's shoulders. On the right is the high mountain wall. On the left is a steep drop-off into space guarded only by a low cable strung along the very edge of the cliff. Cars are slammed here and there against the mountainside. Occasionally, through the hurling snow, I see a car tumbled down the slope of the mountain and crusted into a large boulder.

Back and forth, back and forth our car slides, barely missing disaster. It is impossible to hold back the cries of terror. Finally we reach the bottom of the mountain and Daddy pulls up to a tall brick hotel.

"There is one room left," the manager says. Mom brings in a pile of blankets from the car. She nestles Sarah, the twins and me onto a makeshift bed on the floor. Erla crawls into bed with Mom and Dad. As I drop off to sleep I hear Daddy speaking to Mom in German. "It was the LORD GOD in Heaven who has brought us down the mountainside safely," he says. "Let us thank Him."

Epilogue:

Several weeks later we received word that Grandpa Diener had died. Daddy traveled by bus back to Illinois. However, the bus was delayed and he missed the funeral. Daddy's friend Joe had a car and searched all the small towns until he found Daddy. They rushed to the graveyard, but Grandpa Diener had already been lowered into the ground. The men pulled him back up, opened the casket, and Daddy wept over his departed father.

Worldliness

I am timid. I sit quietly with my head down and my hands folded on my lap. The overstuffed leather couch that my brother, sisters and I are sitting on is crowded. We are in the living room of the *Dawdy Haus* and the room is full of old folks sitting on the straight-backed chairs that have been shoved tightly against one another. They are talking quietly in German about my older cousins.

"Menno's girls are so tall."

"Yes, but they are nice looking."

"But they are so worldly!"

"They wear bandannas!"

"I don't see why Menno allows it."

As I listen to the soft chatter I ponder the meaning of worldliness and wonder what a bandanna is!

We have just arrived in Illinois for Grandpa Diener's household sale. When we pull into the drive I see an older English cousin whose parents had never joined the Amish church. He's harnessed to a buggy and giving rides to younger cousins. Daddy slowly maneuvers the car around them. I press my face into the window and gawk. The small picketed yard surrounding the house is swarming with girls and small children. Older boys come tumbling out of the barn and swarm around our car. There are only fifty-two grandchildren! A sharp-tongued Aunt comes hustling out of the house.

"What are you going to do with all these children?" she demands of Daddy. "You can't let them run around here. There are too many piles of the things for them to get into."

"Well," Daddy replies calmly as he gazes past her into the yard already full of small cousins. "I certainly can't take them back to Pennsylvania, can I?"

"You can't let them run around here!" she says as she turns and hurries back into the house.

So we quietly follow Mom through the crowd of children that has gathered around us as we go into the house. The kitchen and dining room floors are full of large piles of household items. Pots, pans, dishes, towels, sheets, quilts, carpets, etc. are all evenly divided into piles. Each pile has a number printed on a small piece of paper lying on top of it. The aunts and uncles are getting ready to draw numbers to receive the corresponding pile. We are put on the over-stuffed couch in the *Dawdy Haus* among the old folks.

Suddenly, two tall girls with scarves on their heads walk past the living room windows.

"There they are now," someone declares. All heads turn and gaze. The girls enter the front door. They politely go around the room shaking hands and greeting everyone. Then the tall girls take us gently by the hand and lead us out into the yard, through the garden paths, and into the orchard which leads to their farm. We stop in the barn and watch another cousin milk a goat before going into the house. The tall girls remove our wraps and give us warm goat's milk and cookies. All afternoon and evening they play games and read stories to us. I watch in awe. The older folks had said they were "worldly." I figured out the bandanna thing on their heads, but "worldly," what is that? If these tall cousins of mine with bandannas on their heads are worldly, then surely it is something very, very good!

Dawdy's Lydie

I've always loved Dawdy's Lydie. Maybe it's because everyone tells me I look like her. Maybe it's because she's the youngest of my aunts and stayed home and cared for my Mommie and Dawdy (that's Dutch for grandma and grandpa). Dawdy's Lydie is always there when we go to Dawdy's house.

Of course, I don't remember much, 'cause I was only four when we left Illinois and moved to Pennsylvania. But I know I love her and know who she is whenever Mom reads her letters to us.

"Come, Annie," Mom says when she writes to Dawdy's Lydie. I run and climb into Mom's big lap and she guides my hand while I write, "I Love You."

Maybe I love her because every time we return to Illinois to visit Dawdy, Dawdy's Lydie is there. She's very kind and gentle, and I feel very special.

"Come, Annie," Dawdy's Lydie says. She takes me by my hand and guides me up the steep narrow staircase to her room.

She cleans my ears with a big hair pin, then gives me a penny or a piece of candy.

DAWDY'S LYDDIE

After Mommie and Dawdy die, Dawdy's Lydie marries a man from southern Indiana with five children. My contact with her decreases, but she remains "Dawdy's Lydie" and very special to me. As I mature I'm pleased that I look more and more like her.

"Oh," a little child ran up to me, "There's another lady in there," she said, pointing toward the building, "that looks just like you!"

Sure enough, I found my beloved Auntie surrounded by many cousins. When I returned home I pulled out the "Diener

Book" and began counting my Diener cousins. Fifty-three cousins to share my beloved Auntie with!

Dawdy's Lydie died the fall of 2003. She was almost ninety. My brother Lester and I had visited her in her home in Florida seven months before. We were warned that she didn't remember anyone. But, to our surprise, she remembered both of us and chatted about her childhood and told us things that were true.

"My mind is getting worser and worser, but my forgetter is getting better and better!" she said over and over again with a chuckle. My precious "Dawdy's Lydie" will hold a special spot in my heart forever.

Mint Tea

It's fall. It's rainy. Our large brick house with its tall ceilings has become damp and chilly.

"I'm cold," I whine and cling to Mom's apron. If it's not me crying, it's one of the others. Mom finds it hard to move around her large kitchen with us clinging to her, but she manages to build a small fire in the large cast-iron range.

"Hush," Mom says as she fills the teakettle with water and sets it on the old cook stove. She places the heavy butcher knife in the large white round dishpan. "I'm going to fetch tea," she says. We follow her to the front door of the entryway. I press my nose against the cool panels of the fancy cut glass and watch Mom go over the fieldstone pathway, through the rose arbor, and disappear down the long lane toward the forest. The tea grows luscious and tall in the damp ditch along the field. By the time I see Mom returning I hear the whistle of the teakettle in the kitchen.

Mom hustles into the house. She washes the tea and places the leafy stems into the large galvanized tea pot, then pours boiling water over it. We gather around the little worktable, watching and waiting eagerly. Soon the fragrance of the freshly cut mint fills the room.

"I'm going to the springhouse," Mom says, "to fetch cream." She picks up the little cream pitcher and hurries out the back door. I stand on my tiptoes, press my nose against the cool glass of the door and watch Mom go down the steep porch steps and follow the worn path into the deep springhouse. Its spring bubbles up from the ground and fills the cooling troughs with its gentle motion. Then it flows out and joins the small creek at the edge of the backyard. The spring has been bubbling cool fresh water since even before white men came to the mountains. It is the only refrigerator Mom has. I run back to the little table when Mom steps out of the spring house and closes the door behind her.

"She's coming," I announce.

Mom pours the brewed tea into our tin cups, stirs in a spoonful of sugar and adds lots of cream. The aroma is warm and soothing. Many hands reach out eagerly to receive their warm tin cups of freshly brewed spearmint tea. I curl my cold fingers around my cup and pull it close. The fragrance of the creamy sweetness fills the room and gladdens my heart.

Epilogue

Looking back, after brewing many cups of fresh mint tea for my own children I realize that the extra effort of brewing the fresh tea with sweet cream from the deep spring house spelled L-O-V-E.

Evidence of Disobedience

The old-fashioned cast-iron cook stove is raging hot. Popcorn is flying in every direction. My older sister, Sarah, is frantically trying to replace the lid. The shrieks of my sister and the flying corn frighten me. My younger brother and sisters and I huddle tightly into a corner of the darkening room. We are in trouble and we know it.

A storm is blowing in upon our hollow from higher regions. Mom has gone to town with Daddy and Moses to buy supplies before the roads completely close up.

"I've stoked the fire in the basement and in the kitchen stove," Mom says before she leaves. "Don't add more wood, and don't cook any food."

We play contentedly all afternoon. I feel secure in my older sister's care. But now it is getting dark. The fires have both gone out, and the folks aren't home. The house is rapidly growing cold.

"I'm hungry," I whine. "I want popcorn."

"Yes! Yes! Popcorn!" the others chirp.

"No," Sarah says. "We're not to build a fire or cook." I break into a torrent of tears. Soon the others are crying too. So, Sarah lifts the round lid off the stove top. I wipe my tears on my sleeves and hand Sarah two small logs. Then she bends over the wood box, scoops up a dipper of small kindling, and drops it over the logs. I get excited and dance around when she strikes the match on the edge of the stove. It burst into a tiny flame. She lays it on top of the kindling. After the flame takes hold she lays a third log on top of the kindling, just like Mom does. We huddle around the stove, but the crying continues.

"Popping corn isn't *cooking*," I wail. The others join me as I beg and whine. Finally, Sarah sets the heavy old-fashioned crank popcorn popper on the stovetop. The whining stops.

Excitedly we gather around Sarah as she stretches onto her tippy-toes, grabs the handle of the popper and turns the crank.

"Oh! Goodie!" I exclaim when the lard begins to sizzle.

Ker-pop! Ker-pop! Ker-pop! I jump with glee as the kettle begins to fill. Suddenly, the lid slides off the popper and the popping corn flies into the air. I scream, then scamper with the others after the falling corn. Sarah tries to replace the lid, but the pot empties itself onto the floor. Then the folks come home and the evidence of our disobedience cannot be hidden.

"That's OK," Mom says to Sarah, who's sitting on a chair weeping. "The storm moved in ahead of us and we were held up. You did the best you could."

Obedience

Daddy is having difficulty making ends meet on his hilly, rock-strewn farm that's located on the cold side of the mountain slope. The contrast between this farm and the flat fertile plains of Illinois is too great. To supplement his income, Daddy becomes a

Vigertone Salesman. Vigertone is a feed supplement sold to farmers.

Daddy gets up early in the morning to do his own chores and fieldwork before making his rounds to the local farmers. I cry. I don't see much of Daddy anymore as he goes further and further away. Sometimes he's gone several days at a time, or he comes home after I'm in bed and is gone before I'm up in the morning. I cry. I want my Daddy.

"Quit crying," Mom says, "your Daddy has spoiled you rotten!" But I can't quit crying.

One time Daddy is gone for three days and comes home in the middle of the night. By daybreak he's up working in the fields. At noon I still haven't seen my Daddy. The table is set and the dinner is hot and waiting.

"I want you to wait quietly at your places at the table," Mom says as she thoroughly scrubs each one of us. When it's my turn I feel like a baby kitten being rough-handled by its mama. "Your father will soon be in from the fields," Mom says as she turns back to the stove. I can hardly wait. I chatter non-stop.

After a while I hear the tractor coming into the barnyard. In my excitement I scramble to my feet as my chair clatters to the floor. I forget what Mom has said. I guess the others do, too, for we rush out the front door like a herd of cattle, down the steps of the fieldstone front porch, over the curved stone walk with the funny fossils in it, through the rose arbor and into the arms of Daddy! He picks us up one at a time and hugs and kisses us. I don't care that he's sweaty, dusty, and dirty from the fields. He sweeps toddler Erla into his arms and heads for the basement entrance. The rest of us scamper around him like a litter of puppies, happily chattering like squirrels.

When we enter, we are met by an angry Mom standing on the stair steps leading to the dining room. Her hands are propped on her hips with the razor strap across one arm. She hands the strap to Daddy, takes Erla, then demands Daddy to whip the rest of us for leaving the table. The joy of Daddy's arrival fades, but deep in my heart I know it is Mom and not Daddy who whips us that day.

Epilogue

Thirty-five years later the Vigertone Company honored their first salespeople. They searched for Andy Diener and finally found him on a hog farm in northern Indiana during his retirement years. A sad note—the company had found one of his brothers earlier, but he told the representative he didn't know an Andy Diener.

"God will make everything right at the resurrection," Daddy said quietly when he told me about it. That's what Daddy says about any abuse or misunderstandings in life.

Throwing Up

"Well, I declare!" Mom says as she looks up from the *Budget*, which she's been reading all evening. Daddy's working on his farm records at the tall desk in the entryway, which opens into the living room where Mom is reading. We are quietly playing with tinker toys around Mom's rocker.

"Jake Miller's Susie is getting married!" Mom says, "It doesn't seem as if she would be old enough!" I look up and see an amazement on Mom's face.

"Pick up your toys," Mom says as she hurriedly folds the *Budget* and lays it on the rocking chair as she gets up. "It's time for bed."

We follow Mom into the kitchen. She washes our hands and faces then gives us sips of warm milk from a tin cup.

"I don't feel good," I whine.

"Lester," Mom says. "Go to the basement and fetch the large coal bucket." She herds the rest of us up the stairs and tucks us into cool beds. I squirm around until the bed warms up and then drop off to sleep.

"Mommy!" I cry as I sit up in bed. The room is dark and cool, but my bed has become cozy and warm. I don't notice the warmth 'cause my stomach is churning.

"Mommy! Mommy!" Mom grabs me by the arm and pulls me out into the large hallway. She bends me over the big black coal bucket. I hear the others stirring and whimpering. Mom yanks them out of bed and soon we're all crowded around the big old bucket, gagging and throwing up.

The next morning I am sick. I lay in bed and cry. Mom brings me a bowl of hot sweetened milk poured over soda crackers. (That's what you feed babies and old people who don't have teeth.)

"Eat it," Mom says. I eat it and continue to cry. Mom tries all her home remedies, but nothing helps.

"Guess I'll have to call the doctor," Mom says.

"Oh," I moan after Mom leaves the room. If the doctor is coming I must be very sick. I'll probably not live much longer. In distress I roll out of bed and pace the floor. I stop and gaze out the window. The large barn door on the other side of the tall hedge is rolled back several feet. Our German Shepherd dog, followed by her large litter of puppies, comes out of the barn.

"Oh," I burst into tears, "I'll probably not live long enough to see the puppies grow up." I crawl back into bed and pull the covers over my head. I have no choice but to accept my fate.

Finally the doctor arrives. He is carrying a little black bag. "Open your mouth," he says, "and say AHHH." He holds my tongue down with a flat stick. I gag. I can't say anything. He asks several questions and then takes hold of my wrist and starts counting. What is he counting? He pulls a strange- looking thing out of his bag. It has three tubes hooked together. He puts two ends in his ears and holds the third to my chest. He counts again. Then he puts it on my stomach and listens. What does he hear? I squeeze my eyes shut to hold back the tears. Surely I will not live much longer. He puts the tube back into his bag and pulls out a large bottle of medicine and pours a little into a smaller bottle.

"Give her a teaspoon of this and she'll be feeling fine in a short time," the doctor says. He hands the little bottle to Mom. They walk out the door. I hear them talking as they go down the stairs. I get up and quietly slip to the window. I watch the doctor crawl into his car, turn it around, and disappear down the lane. I crawl back into bed.

Mom comes into my room with the little bottle and a spoon.

"Open," she says as she pours the first dose of medicine into the spoon and then down my throat. Sure enough, it's just as the doctor had said. Within a very short time I feel perky again and am outside playing with the puppies!

Epilogue

I've never been able to figure out how my mother rallied us all around that big old coal bucket for one big throw-up party instead of several individual ones. My own children never cooperated in such matters. They preferred individual attention, especially at night.

Cold Feet!

My feet are freezing! The car is cold, and as usual, I am crying.

"Annie," Mom says as she turns from the front seat, "sit back. You're making a bigger fuss than all the others put together."

Strong winds are roaring through the mountain passes. We've been caught in a blizzard that is blowing down upon us from the higher Allegheny peaks of Pennsylvania. Daddy stopped while we were yet on the hard road and put the chains on the wheels. But they aren't helping now. Deep drifts have filled in the low ridges of our mile-long lane. The lane climbs up and down and in and out among boulders and trees that separate our farm from the paved road.

"Sit back!" Mom says to me. She's getting stern. "If your feet are cold sit on them!"

"How can I sit on my feet? They're on the floor and I'm on the seat!"

"Dumb!" Moses turns around from the front seat beside Mom. He points a crooked finger into my face.

"Dumb Annie!" I burst into tears. I try to do as the others are doing, but the seat is crowded, my legs are stiff, and my feet are numb.

"I guess we better walk home before the storm gets worse," Daddy says as he opens the car door. He's been examining the situation outside. He hands little Erla to Moses and picks up both twins in his arms while Mom takes Sarah and me by the hand. We begin the long trudge through the snow. Not a sound is heard except the crunch of our feet, the strong winds twirling and howling around us, and the sobbing of my tightening chest.

I'm happy when we come around the last curve and the house and barn come into view. "The fire in the furnace has gone out," Daddy observes from the smokeless chimney. When we arrive he goes to the basement to stoke the furnace while Mom takes our coats, boots and shoes off. She wraps us in cold quilts then plops us onto the tall radiator along the dining room wall. It's cold too. My brothers, sisters and I shiver until our teeth rattle inside our cold cocoon of quilts.

"Annie, quit crying!" Mom says every few minutes. "Crying doesn't help! Quit it!" Mom hustles to get a fire going in the kitchen stove. About the time I begin to feel whisks of heat on the radiator Mom brings cups of warmed milk. Warmth radiates up around us as we sit on the radiator with our warm cups of milk cuddled in our hands.

When the hot water reservoir on the ceiling above the upstairs bathtub is warm, Mom fills the tub and puts us into it. She warms our beds by wrapping heated bricks in towels and placing them under the covers. Then, one by one, she dresses us in our feed sack gowns and tucks us into warmed up beds. The shivering stops, but as I drift off to sleep, I am still pondering the mystery of how to sit on my own feet.

I Love God's Word

A calendar hangs by the small mirror on the dining room wall beside the stairway door. The step beneath the door helps me see the tiny words on the calendar. On the other side of the mirror is a small shelf on which Daddy keeps his strap, razor and a tin cup full of shaving soap. The calendar is not an ordinary one. It has a special Bible verse printed on it for each day. I frequently stop beneath it during the day and try to read the tiny words. Even though I've been in school for several years, I cannot read.

Daddy talks out loud to himself all the time. So, when he reads and rereads the verse while he is shaving, I stand on the step and listen. I try to repeat the verse with him.

"Annie," Mom calls from the kitchen. "It's your turn to set the table." I hurry to the kitchen and grab a stack of bowls. I keep my eye on Daddy and the calendar while I quickly place a bowl at each place, then hop up on the step by the mirror. Daddy looks down and smiles. He looks funny with soap lather spread across his face.

"Annie!" Mom's forceful voice makes me jump. I run into the kitchen and grab a handful of spoons. Clang! Clang! Clang! I toss a spoon carelessly into each tin bowl.

"Annie!" Mom's instructive voice stops me. "Be neat!" Tears gather in my eyes. Daddy is done shaving, and I haven't learned the verse.

After supper during the long dark winter nights, Daddy fetches the big Bible Story Book from the living room. He sits on a chair in the kitchen under the flickering glow of the kerosene lantern that hangs from a hook in the middle of the ceiling. It casts large eerie shadows throughout the room. The Bible Story Book has pictures in it. The younger ones crowd around Daddy's knees while we older ones help Mom wash the dishes.

"Come on, Annie, bring the dirty dishes," Mom urges when it is my turn to clear the dining room table. Reluctantly, I pull away from Daddy's chair and run into the dining room. With each load I stop to take a peek and stay until I'm called away.

"Annie, that dish is dry," Mom scolds when it is my turn with the dishtowel. I'm standing by the open Bible Story Book with the towel going round and round an already dry dish.

"Come on, Annie." Mom hurries me along on the nights it's my turn to put the dried dishes away. "Come on, the counter is full, we need more room!"

And so, on long winter nights at the foot of Mount Davis, Daddy instills in me a love for God's Word, while Mom teaches me to be responsible within the family unit.

Snowed In

"Aw," Mom says as she walks into the girls' bedroom and looks out the window. "This is the closest thing to the world stopping and letting us get off. No school today, girls!" I sit up in bed. The wind is howling around the large four-story brick house. I shiver. "Don't worry," Mom says. "We've plenty of everything we need. Our coal bins are full and the cellars are stocked."

"But the puppies in the barn will get cold," I say as I look out the window.

"They're OK," Mom says. "The barn is cozy." In my mind's eye I see steam rising off the backs of animals and hear the cackle of the hens in the chicken house.

I roll out of bed, run to the window and press my face against the cold windowpane to get a closer look. Large drifts of snow are piling up everywhere. The tall hedge between the house and barn has almost disappeared. "Wow!" I exclaim as I pull away, dress quickly, and follow Mom as she does her morning chores.

In a few days the sun is shining again in the crystal blue skies.

"Let's build a big, tall snowman!" Lester says.

"Goodie! Goodie!" I say as I jump up and down. Mom herds us down the basement steps and bundles us up.

"Don't stay long," Mom says as she herds us out the basement door. The snow sparkles and dances before my eyes. Even though I know it won't work, I try to scoop up a mittenfull of sparkles, but they dance away. I see Lester rolling a large ball. I grab up a handful of snow, pat it firmly, then roll it through the fluffy snow. I look behind me and see the curvy uneven path my snow ball is making. Soon it becomes so big I can't push it.

"Lester," I call, "Come and help me!" We place it on top of his bigger ball. Before long a tall snowman stands on the slope of the backyard. He has two chunks of coal for eyes, a corn cob nose, and branchy sticks for arms.

I see my sister making a snow angel. I throw myself backwards onto a snow drift, extend my arms above my head then bring them down along my side. Soon a group of serene snow angles surrounds our snowman as he stands on the hillside looking into our windows.

"Annie!" Mom says as she helps me crawl out of my snow-covered wraps. We're down in the basement. "Stop crying!" She herds us up the stairs and plops us one by one on top of the warm dining room register. "Stop crying! You'll soon be warm."

I look at the others sitting on the register beside me. They're not crying. Mom's gone to the kitchen. I smell warm soothing cocoa heating on the old cast-iron cook stove. I wipe my face on my sleeve and wait.

"Here you are," Mom says as she bustles into the room with steaming cups in a large pie pan. I cuddle mine in my hands and sip slowly.

"How about some popcorn?" Daddy calls into the kitchen as he pulls out the long bench from under the table and sets up the checkerboard on it. "No one in this house can beat me at checkers!" He hops up onto the other end, flops his arms, crows like a rooster, then somersaults to the floor and stands on his head.

"I beat ya! I beat ya!" Many little voices chirp as they slide off the tall radiator and crowd around Daddy and his checkerboard.

More Snow

"I'll shovel a path to the barn," Moses says to Daddy as he stands at the entryway window with his legs apart and his hands propped on his hips. The howling winds from the high Allegheny ranges are stacking drifts of snow between the house and the barn. I press my face against the cold windowpane of the cut glass front door and peer out into the thrilling whiteness. An excited shiver runs through my body. It's spooky to hear the wind howl around the large four-story brick house and watch high snow drifts stack up higher and higher.

I follow Daddy and the others to the basement, slip into my boots and barn wraps, then follow Daddy to the barn. I whimper as a strong blast of wind throws me off balance.

"Annie, you coming?" Daddy turns and waits. When we get to the barn Daddy slides the big heavy door back a bit and we slip in. It's a cozy place. The hay mows and silos are stacked full and the animals are content in their stalls. There's a sour-sweet smell and wisps of steam evaporating from their bodies. We do our assigned chores and soon it is time to return to the house. The newly dug path has filled with snow. Moses empties the path again as we follow the slow progression toward the house. I cling tightly to my coat. The strong wind isn't friendly as it hoots and howls and grabs at my wraps.

By morning the snow is stacked high in the hollow between the house and barn.

"I know what I'll do," Moses says, "I'll dig a tunnel"

"I like Moses' tunnel," I say after I've run through it several times, but Mom and Daddy look funny—they have to stoop.

"Let's go sledding," Daddy says when the sun shines again. I run to the basement with the others and crawl into my heavy winter wraps.

"Here," Mom says as she comes down the steps, "let me see if you are bundled up well." When Mom's done it's hard to walk.

"Let's do it again," I say every time the sled comes to a slow stop. When we hear the whistle blow we know it's time to hurry to the house.

"Stop crying, Annie," Mom says as she peels away the cold wet outer garments, herds us up the stairs and plops us on top of the tall register in the dining room. "You'll soon be warm." Mom lifts the corner of her apron and wipes my tears, then picks up the large white dishpan with the red rim around the edge and heads out the back door.

"Yippee!" I yell as we slide off the tall register and scurry to shove the large heavy dining room chairs into a large circle. Mom returns with apples from the deep cellar. We sit on the chairs around her rocker, waiting our turn for a *snitch* (a slice of apple).

"Annie, hold still—be quiet," Mom says. "You'll get your turn. Annie, stop it."

After supper I hear Mom whipping a bowl of whipped cream.

"Yeah! Yeah!" I yell and run into the kitchen. Mom is laying the beater into the sink. She slips into her winter wraps, picks up the large dish pan and steps out the back door. Many faces press against the cold window pane as we watch Mom scoop up gallons of freshly fallen snow.

"Snow ice cream!" I squeal and twirl. "It's yum, yummy for the tummy!" When Mom comes in she quickly folds in the flavored whipped cream. I can almost taste it before she hands me my bowl.

Frolicking

"Andy," Mom calls to Daddy. "We've come through several days of blizzards and the snow is stacked high. I'm tired of being snowed in—I'd like to see other faces for a change."

"Well," Daddy says, " I think the tractor could take us across the fields to Bakers'."

"Oh, goodie!" The other children and I dance around Mom.

"Hush!" Mom says as she turns back to Daddy. "I'll pop a lard can full of popcorn to take along."

"Yippee!" I yell.

"Annie! Control yourself," Mom says as she pushes me aside and heads for the kitchen. I follow Daddy down the basement steps and watch him get into his high boots and wraps.

When I return to the kitchen the five-gallon lard tin is almost full of popcorn. I "snitch" a handful and run to the glass cut door in the front entry and watch Daddy back the tractor up to the little alcove. Mom sets the filled can next to the door, grabs my shoulder and pulls me into the dining room. The radiator is piled high with our winter wraps. As Mom bundles me, I'm engulfed in the warmth of the radiator. Daddy picks me up and places me beside the others on the back of the platform. Mom inspects us carefully and then climbs on with the lard can full of corn.

"OOH!" my eyes get big as the tractor plows through deep drifts, causing loose clouds of snow flurries to float in the air around us. Soon we are covered with fluffy snow. We yelp, holler and sing. I'm sure the Bakers Clan can hear us coming.

When we reach the steepest hill in the last field, the can of popcorn slides off the platform.

"Stop!" everyone yells. I'm laughing so hard I almost roll off too.

"I'll get it!" Lester says as he slides off the platform and rolls down the hillside to retrieve the can. When he returns he looks like a snowman. The tractor's front wheels tip into the air and dance like a bulking horse when Daddy starts the tractor again, so he backs down to the bottom, turns the tractor around and slowly backs up the hill. We "Ooh," "Ah," shout and holler.

When we finally make it to the Baker home the large family is gathered around the table eating a meal of green bean soup. Everyone is glad to see us.

The men and boys go out on the hillside to ski while we girls slide down the slopes on a toboggan. The men and boys whoop and holler. They're making an awful lot of noise. The women are enjoying a quiet time alone, that is, until the energetic noise comes back into the house.

"Ha! Ha! Ha!"

"You should have seen Andy!"

"Ha! Ha! Ha!" The men and boys are laughing and jostling each other. They look like jolly snowmen, all talking at once. I shiver as I listen to them. I'm wet and cold.

"Andy fell headfirst into a snow bank. You should have seen him!"

"His legs and skies dangled upside down in the air." Daddy is laughing too.

"When we pulled him out, he looked like a snowman!"

"It's time to do the evening chores," Daddy says after the laughter dies down. Mom bundles us up, and with our empty tin we pile onto the tractor's platform and head for home.

The Joy of Tobogganing

I'll never forget the winter of the deep snow. The large heavy back wheels of Daddy's little Allis-Chalmers tractor grip through the drifts as he hauls the cans of cream to the road once a week and brings back the collected mail.

"We have a surprise for you," Mom says one evening after she and Daddy poured over the pages of the Sears Roebuck catalog. She folds a piece of paper and places it inside an envelope. Daddy goes to the tall desk and gets a three-cent stamp.

"But," Mom says, "you must wait until it comes."

"What is it? What is it?" I squeal as I jump up and down. Lydie and Lester and the others are standing patiently by the table.

"Annie, you must wait until it comes," Mom smiles at me. And so, I wait and wait and wait. Then I wait and wait some more. The waiting seems forever.

Finally, after several weeks, Daddy returns with a long, narrow package.

"What is it? What is it?" I screech and bounce up and down. The twins stand patiently by as Daddy inspects the package and turns it over. I cannot contain the excitement swelling within me. Slowly and carefully, Daddy begins to unwrap the mysterious long package. I cannot believe my eyes!

"It's a toboggan!" We squeal and jump up and down. "It's like the one the Baker's have!" I exclaim.

"This will hold all of us," Daddy says, "if we double-deck." After eating a quick lunch Mom bundles us up and we head for the long sloping field above the barn. The fences and hedges are under snow. The sun is shining brightly. Its rays dance like sparkling crystals in every direction around me; as usual, I try to gather some into my gloves.

"Dumb Annie!" Moses says. I ignore him.

Daddy and Moses make the virgin run on the toboggan. When they arrive back at the top of the slope we all clamber to pile on.

"You older ones hold the younger ones," Daddy says as he settles us each in place. Daddy gives us a running push, then hops on in a standing position with his feet tucked under Mom. About halfway down the hill Daddy whoops and hollers. I turn and see him roll into the snow. On each run Daddy gains better control and soon we are buzzing past the barn, across the road, and then halting halfway through the flat field that runs by the edge of the forest.

Mom's children are a jabbering, rosy-cheeked bunch that gather around her supper table that evening. While the dishes are being washed Daddy sits in the middle of the kitchen under the hanging lantern and reads to us a Bible story, then Mom tucks us into warmed beds. Sleep comes quickly. I drop into a deep sleep and dream of another adventurous day surrounded by the sparkling crystals of the snow on the sunny slopes with our new beloved toboggan.

Treadle Sewing Machine

"Mom," I say, "I want to sew! Please, let me sew." I'm standing behind Mom's treadle sewing machine, pressing my face as close to the needle as I can. I'm intrigued as the needle hurriedly plunges up and down through the feed sack material Mom is guiding underneath the little metal foot. A straight line of stitches stretches out behind it as her foot rhythmically pumps the treadle up and down. "Please, Mom, let me try."

"No," Mom says. "You're too young. You need to wait several years." She pushes her chair back, gets up and heads toward the kitchen.

"Come, girls," Mom calls. "The men folks will be in soon." I reluctantly follow and stand in the doorway.

"Annie, you set the table. Sarah, you slice the bread. Lydie, you fill the water glasses." With each trip into the dining room I stop briefly at the sewing machine. When I'm finished I return to the sewing machine, but no matter how I position myself on the chair, I cannot reach the treadle with my feet and guide the material under the needle at the same time.

"Lester," I call to my younger brother who's playing nearby. "Come pump the treadle for me. I want to sew like Mom does." Lester comes and flops on the floor on the other side of the machine. Without warning the needle takes off at a fast clip. My fingers try to keep up with the curvy trail the stitches are making in the piece of material Mom has been working on.

PLOP! The machine comes to a sudden halting stop as the needle plunges deep into my finger. A wail arises that brings the whole household running. Blood is splattering and flowing onto Mom's freshly bleached project. Quickly Mom releases the pressure foot and removes the needle from my finger. She drags me up the stairs to the bathroom, disinfects my finger and wraps it in a clean rag.

It is a sober, subdued Annie that comes down the stairs to the dinner table that day. I hold my wrapped injured finger in my other hand.

"Dumb!" Moses says, looking straight at me. "Dumb Annie!" I burst into tears.

"It was Lester's fault," I exclaim as I stare in his direction.

"No," Mom says. "It was your fault. I told you to leave the sewing machine alone." Seven pairs of accusing eyes turn toward me.

"Dumb Annie!" Moses says as he points a crooked finger from across the table. I drop my head and let the tears flow.

"Annie! Sit up and eat," Mom says sternly, but I cannot eat. All I can do is cry. Daddy picks me up and lays me on the couch in the living room. I hold my finger tightly and I sob myself to sleep.

Winter Evenings

The winter evenings are dark and long. Daddy reads Bible stories to us while we clean up the kitchen. Then Mom pulls the old wicker rocker under the kerosene lamp that hangs from a hook on the dining room ceiling. She piles a heap of socks that need mending into her lap. Daddy has his farm magazine spread out on the dining room table. He makes funny sounds through his teeth as he reads.

"Let's play hide-n-go seek," Lester says. "I'll be 'it!'"

"Mom, help me hide," I say as I crawl under her apron and nestle into her big lap. She piles the socks around me and keeps on mending. The others hustle here and there until they all disappear.

"Coming! Ready or not!" Lester calls. Mom lays her head back and laughs till the tears come as each one of us is found. Then she lays her mending aside, gets up, and helps us hide again. Poor Mom, she doesn't get much mending done when we play hide-n-go-seek.

"How about some popcorn?" Daddy asks. I follow Mom into the kitchen. She pulls out the banged-up crank popcorn popper, dips in a measure of lard, then sets it on the stove. When the lard sizzles Mom pours in the kernels.

"Ker-Pop! Ker-Pop!" The kernels begin to dance in the kettle, and I dance and twirl around Mom.

"Annie! Stop it!" Mom says when I dive under her apron in an attempt to imitate the popping corn. All of Mom's children are anxiously popping around her like the kernels in the pan.

"Let's play Bible Travel Log," Daddy calls from the dining room.

"Oh! Goodie! Goodie!" I exclaim. "That's my favorite game!"

Mom carries the big heaping pan full of corn to the dining room table. I grab a handful and watch Daddy open the board. Mom reads the Bible questions and Daddy helps us find the answers. Then we get to move forward a few spaces. When my turn is over, I dive back into the pan of corn for another handful and stuff it into my mouth.

"Annie!" Mom scolds, "You're not a pig! Eat slower!"

"Who wants to play me a game of checkers?" Daddy asks after we've finished our game. He reaches for his pocket watch and flips the lid open. "Yep," he says as he flips the lid shut again and stuffs it back into his pocket. "There's still time for a good game of checkers!" I love it when Daddy plays checkers. It doesn't matter that he beats us all the time. What matters is the exuberant show that follows.

"No one can beat me in checkers," Daddy declares as he jumps up on his chair and stretches his short stocky self to the fullest of his height. He flaps his arms and crows like a rooster and then somersaults to the floor and stands on his head.

Mom gets up and begins to carry chairs into the cool dark parlor. Daddy carries in the light. He, Mom, Moses and Sarah go into the room and close the door. They are going to worship God. We little ones are still too young. We huddle outside the door, and I listen intently, trying to catch a word or two as it floats through the heavy wooden door. I hear the chairs shuffle as they drop to their knees. Then the long prayer in Daddy's sing-song German voice begins. I wish I was old enough to worship God.

Epilogue:

I didn't know how much my Mom gave of herself in those long ago snowed-in days until I had children of my own. Then my respect for Mom rose considerably. I can still hear the ring of her jolly laughter as she laid her head back against the rocker and laughed until the tears came. Yes, on those cold winter days my mother gave of her fullest to the young family around her.

Homemade Ice Cream

"What ya doing?" I ask Daddy as I skip down the cellar steps into the large walk-in basement. The chores are done and Daddy is crawling into his heavy barn wraps again. The severe storm has finally blown itself out after several days of howling around the four corners of our large four-story brick house, and the sun is shining brightly on the beautiful freshly-painted mountain landscape.

"The buckets of water I set outside this morning are frozen," Daddy says. "I'm going to dump them into this gurney bag and crush them." Daddy picks up the heavy sledgehammer and the gurney sack and steps outside. I push a wooden box over to the window in time to see Daddy lift the heavy sledge up over his head with both hands and bring it down on the bulky bag full of the frozen chucks. With each blow the bag becomes flatter. Surely there is no Daddy as strong as mine.

"Mom! Mom!" I squeal as I rush up the stairs. "Daddy is crushing ice. He's going to make ice cream!"

"I know," Mom says as she turns slightly toward me. She's whipping eggs into a large pan of milk.

"Oh! Goodie!" I squeal and race into the living room where the others are playing. "We're going to make ice cream!" I announce proudly. There's a sudden stamp of feet down the cellar steps followed by Mom carrying the metal container full of the flavored milk. She places it into the tall wooden freezer tub and Daddy fills the sides with layers of crushed ice and salt, then secures the crank in place and folds a burlap bag on top.

"My turn! My turn!" Many little voices chirp to crank the handle. After many turns and much cranking, the ice cream begins to freeze and the cranking becomes harder.

"Here, Lester," Daddy calls to my brother, "come sit on the freezer so I can crank it some more." Lester is the only one heavy enough to hold the freezer steady. I jump and squeal with glee when the crank won't go any more. Daddy gets up and begins removing the melted ice off the top of the freezer.

"Goodie! Goodie!" I twirl and dance. "It's done! It's done!"

"Annie," Mom says, "contain yourself. You act as if you've never had ice cream before."

Daddy wipes the salt off the lid, slowly opens it, and hands it to Mom. The first glimpse makes my eyes bulge; I lick my lips—I can taste it already. I watch as Daddy slowly pulls up the dasher and lays it on a cookie sheet. We grab a spoon and lick it clean, then Daddy carries the container to the kitchen.

"Here, Annie," Mom says as she hands me a bowl of soft, fluffy goodness. I love to feel its smooth, cool, sweetness slide down my throat. After the two-gallon container is empty, I'm stuffed. A shiver runs down my spine, then another and another one. I shove a chair to the tall register in the dining room and clamber onto the warmest spot in the house.

Rooster of the Barnyard

"Who wants to beat me at checkers?" Daddy asks as he sets up the checkerboard on the dining room table. We have just finished eating and Mom, my sisters and I are still busy in the kitchen.

"I do!" I yell as I run from the kitchen with a towel and the bowl I am drying.

"Annie!" Mom's voice stops me, "the dishes aren't done yet."

"I'll beat ya!" Lester says as he scoots down the long wooden bench toward Daddy.

During the long winter evenings the checkerboard frequently appears. The board is set up on the dining room table, the library table in the living room, or on a chair under the kitchen lamp while the dishes are being washed. Daddy is the #1 player. He has no mercy on us young'uns, but we don't want it any other way.

I hear a whoop and a holler and a clatter of chairs. I run into the dining room.

"Annie!" Mom's sharp voice stops me. I stand transfixed in the doorway. My sisters crowd in behind me. Daddy leaps onto the bench and flops his arms.

"Cockle-Doodle-Doo," he crows. "No one in this household can beat me in checkers!" He crows again and then, with a dramatic flip-flop, he somersaults to the floor and stands on his head.

"I'll beat ya! I'll beat ya!" many little voices clamber to be next.

Epilogue:

Daddy's undefeated victories continued on into our adult lives. In his retirement years Daddy added chess to his skills. His victories continued until Alzheimer's claimed his mind, then sadly, his grandchildren, whom he had also taught, began beating him at his own game.

Old Enough at Last!

I jump up and down. At last, Mom is placing another chair in the semi-circle of the cool, quiet parlor of the large brick house.

"Is it for me? Is it for me?" I ask excitedly. "Is the chair for me?"

"Yes," Mom says, "it is for you, Annie! But you must sit still and listen. Do not make any noise."

"Tonight!" I say as I turn toward my younger brother and sisters. "I'm going into the room!"

"Come," Mom says to me as she holds the parlor door open. I enter the cool, quiet room and climb onto my assigned chair. I fold my arms tightly against my chest, my short legs sticking straight out in front of me as I sit expectantly beside my older brother and sister.

Daddy places an oil lamp on the little shelf above the library table. It flickers, casting long shadows across the room. I watch as Mom closes the door. I know my younger brother and sisters are huddling quietly on the other side. I am big and important now.

The long awaited moment has finally arrived. Tonight I, too, will worship God!

In the glow of the kerosene lamp Daddy reaches for the large German Bible lying on the library table. A quiet reverence and awe swells within me as his strong, steady voice begins to read. I sit quietly and listen. On the other side of the door my younger brother and sisters can only hear the murmur of his voice, but I can hear each German word distinctly.

Daddy finishes reading and tenderly closes the large Bible. In a slow gentle movement he lays it back on the library table, then picks up the small German Prayer Book. I slide off my chair with the others and kneel on the cool polished hardwood floor.

"*O Du Lieber Gott Vather ins de Himmel. Barmhersiger* (Almighty, Gracious, Righteous, Loving, Heavenly Father in Heaven)," Daddy begins in German. His voice rises and falls rhythmically as the long prayer flows smoothly out of the little Prayer Book. I cannot as yet understand High German, but the seeds of reverent respect are being sown into my life.

I feel content as I return to the younger children. At last, I am old enough to share in the reading of God's Word.

"Surely now," I say to myself, "God will allow me to come to Heaven when I die!"

Sleigh Dogs

"I think this will do," Moses says as he gets up from a pile of leather straps and buckles that are scattered around him. It's Monday morning and I'm down in the basement helping Mom with the weekly wash. The big double-tub washing machine Daddy bought makes washday much easier for Mom.

"Mose," Mom says as he heads towards the cellar door, "you can't leave your mess. Clean up after yourself."

"I'll be back," he says. "I want to see how this fits."

We're snowed in again. No one goes anywhere. Some of Mom's staples are running low. She's stretching them as thin as she can.

"Annie," Mom says as she pushes a low stool toward me, "hang up this little stuff on that line by the window. I'll be back in a minute." She picks up a basket full of wet clothing and follows Moses out the basement door.

Moses and Mom return about the same time.

"They fit," Moses says.

"What fits?" Mom asks as she plunges her cold hands into the warm wash water.

"The harness I'm making for the dogs. I'm going to hook them to the toboggan and go to the Springs store for supplies."

"It won't work," Mom says. "Your dogs aren't trained."

"I'll train them," Moses says.

We crowd around the entryway windows during the next couple of days and watch Moses train his team of dogs. They soon learn to pull together.

"Where's your list?" Moses asks Mom. "I'm heading for the store." An awe arises inside me as we watch Moses and his dogs slide smoothly across the snow-covered fields toward the Tressler farm and the sand quarry. It's further that way, but there are more open fields with less snow.

The afternoon is long. I keep peering out of different windows, hoping for a glimpse of Moses and his dogs. Finally, toward evening they come limping in. One dog is missing, and Mose is in its harness.

"Where's Max?" Dad asks.

"Oh, that dumb dog gave me trouble all the way home. He didn't want to pull. When we got to the sand quarry his harness broke and he took off. I couldn't stop him."

"He'll get cold!" I wail as tears rush down my face.

"Dumb!" Moses turns and snarls at me.

"Stop crying!" Mom says. "Max knows the way home."

But Max doesn't come home. I think of him falling into one of the many deep gullies full of slippery rocks and snow with no food to eat and no way out. Or maybe he's caught in a bear trap. Either way he'll freeze to death. I find a dark corner alone and cry!

Going Through Motions

"Come on, Annie, stop going through the motions and get those dishes clean," Mom scolds. We girls have our assigned clean-up jobs after each meal.

"It's your turn to sweep the floor, Annie," Mom says after all the dishes are neatly stacked in their proper place inside the tall cabinet. "Don't just go through the motions, either. I want every crumb up off the floor, and don't sweep the dirt under the carpet. Use the dust pan. People will think I haven't taught you anything."

Why does Mom scold me so much? I don't hear her talking to my sisters about their work. It seems as if I can't do any job she gives me to her satisfaction.

Each Saturday the house is thoroughly cleaned. Mom always probes and keeps after me to complete my assigned job properly.

"I hate Saturday work!" I grumble to myself. "Why couldn't I have been a boy?" I want to be outside running in the sunshine, climbing trees and jumping in the haymow. Anything would be better than going though the motions of the Saturday morning routine. And now that it is spring, the whole house will be scrubbed from top to bottom.

"I hate it!" I grumble to Mom, "Why does the house need to be scrubbed?"

"Don't ask so many questions. Just do it!" Mom says. Even the attic and basement don't escape Mom's scrutinizing eyes. I hate these weeks of being scolded and probed through scrubbing, polishing and rearranging. The kittens, the puppies and the great out-of-doors keep calling me, but no, I am stuck in the house scrubbing things that don't even look dirty. It makes no sense to me.

"Annie," Mom says, "Don't scrub the wall in tiny circles. Go up and down!" So, I go up and down.

"Annie, you are skipping spots. Go back and forth!" So, I go back and forth.

"Annie, you're making a mess of that wall! Don't just go through the motions! Get it clean!"

My abilities don't seem to improve with age. "It would be easier for me to do this myself," Mom often says. "You go through the motions, but you don't get anything done!"

Epilogue:

When I was fifteen I took the Driver's Education Course in high school. The first thing I failed was removing the hubcap from the wheel.

"You're going though the right motions," the instructor kept saying, but the cap did not come off.

Then, during a snowy blizzard one January morning the State Cop came to give us our final driving examination. I was the last one to be taken out. The streets were closing up fast. When we returned to the school I got stuck in the snow bank as I was attempting to parallel park. I saw my classmates watching from the windows. My heart sank as the policeman crawled out of the passenger side, stomped through the snow and drove the car out of the drift.

I felt dejected as the officer handed out signed driver's licenses to the other students. When he came to me he stopped, rubbed his chin, then grinned as he handed me my license.

"You went through the right motions," he said. "The snow wasn't your fault." A cheer arose from my classmates. We'd passed 100%. I felt great! It was the first time in my life I'd ever been rewarded for "going though the motions!"

I Can't Remember

I do not remember our family moving into Springs, Pennsylvania, even though it is only three miles from the farm, and I'm seven years older than I was when we moved to the farm. It is as if I awoke one morning and there I was! But I do remember our family visiting the Carter family that lived there and playing under the tall front porch with a girl my age. I made a new friend that day and was disappointed when she moved away.

This house has a side basement entry and the tall front porch is surrounded with shrubs. A horseshoe drive enters on one side of the house, circles the back yard and then exits to the road on the other side. Pine trees grow along the outside edge of the lane on the right side of the house.

"I'm going to transplant young pines from the woods," Daddy says as he pulls the truck keys out of his pocket, "then we'll have a windbreak on both sides of the house."

"Can I go? Can I go?" I clutch Daddy's arm and jump up and down in front of him.

"Ask your mother," Daddy says. I make a quick switch and bounce in front of Mom. It isn't long until my brother, sisters and I are bouncing on the back of the truck. We play contentedly in the forest while Daddy digs saplings. When we get home, he plants them along the lane on the one side of the house. They are tiny compared to the half-grown ones lining the other side.

(Neither do I remember the building of the barn, which is a garage, shop, barn and chicken house combination at the top of the horseshoe drive. It's as if that building just appeared. I know Daddy built it because I've seen pictures of the process.)

PENNSYLVANIA FARMHOUSE

Frances, My Good Neighbor

My brother, sisters and I are crowded onto a bench in the home of an older person who has died in Upper Springs. My parents have come to show their respect. The house is full, but there is always room for one more family. The room we are sitting in is quiet except for the whispered murmur of adults discussing the current gossip. An older woman is going to have a baby!

"There she comes," someone whispers, and a strange hush falls across the room. A lady holding the hand of a boy about my age walks into the room, but I do not see a baby. She is followed by a young teenage girl and her husband. After shaking hands with the adults they find a place to sit. The room remains quiet. When my parents come from the viewing room we kids follow single file as they lead us out through the crowded rooms. Mom is full of news concerning the woman and the baby on the way home.

I forget about the incident until after we leave the farm and move to Springs. Then the lady I had seen at the viewing becomes our neighbor across the road. Her name is Frances, and her little son's name is Bobby. I soon discover she is my friend. Her lane makes a long sloping loop along both boundary lines of her and her husband's property. They live in a long narrow house at the bottom of the loop. It had been built as a chicken house, but no chickens ever lived in it. I can close my eyes and see Frances running up the slope of her driveway. She runs everywhere she goes.

"What's wrong, Annie?" Frances asks as I step into her kitchen one day.

"Oh!" I sob and burst into tears. She stops what she's doing and pulls out a chair for me.

"Tell me what is bothering you," Frances says as she sits down beside me and puts an arm around my shoulder. It isn't long until the sun is shining in my heart again as she lends a listening ear and an understanding heart. Frances never tells me to sit down, hold still and be quiet like other adults do. She never thinks that I am in her way or that I ask too many questions.

"How about helping me bake some cookies?" Frances asks. My smile is big and wide. Soon I'm licking a beater and a bowl that doesn't need to be shared. Other days I help her wash dishes or scrub the floor. She has a special way of involving me in whatever she is doing. I love Frances.

Frances and her husband, Phil, always have time to take long walks into the nearby forest with us neighborhood kids. And as we walk we learn about the times, places and people who've lived in these woods before us. They laugh, tease, and teach us names of herbs, rocks, flowers and trees mingled with stories of bygone days.

Epilogue

At the end of my senior year my family moved to Nappanee, Indiana. I missed Frances, but her daughter lived in Fort Wayne, Indiana, so we kept some contact. Whenever I returned to Springs Frances' welcome mat was always out.

"Anna," Frances said, with a faraway look in her eyes. I was spending several days with her. She was almost ninety now. Phil, her husband, had died some years previously. Her youngest son, Bobby, and his wife were living in a trailer parked on one side of the looping driveway of the hillside yard. "Anna," she said again, "years ago, when I got pregnant with Bobby I wondered why I, an older woman, was having another baby. But now I know he was a special gift from God. God knew my older children would move far away, so he sent Bobby to care for me in my old age."

World War II

The siren blows. The long sharp high-pitched shrill sound sends goose bumps down my spin. All heads pop up. The third grade class has been resting while our teacher, Mrs. Livingood, has been reading a story. She reads a chapter each day after the noon recess. Today she stops in the middle of a sentence, closes the book, and lays it on top of her desk. All eyes are glued on her as she picks up the long window stick and glides smoothly down the tall row of windows. Quickly and quietly she pulls down the thick dark black shades. Automatically we disappear under our desks. I roll into a tight ball. Fear grips my chest. It's hard to breathe.

"Are the Germans coming?"

"Will a bomb explode on our school?"

"Are we going to be killed?"

"What will it feel like to die?" I tremble as I wait expectantly. Silent tears flow down my cheeks. The room is deathly quiet. No one moves. The eerie dead quietness sends chills up and down my spine. I wish I knew if it was real or only an exercise.

The sirens that warn us give different messages. During a more urgent and longer warning all three rooms of the large brick elementary school file quickly to the basement in long lines along the walls, then we crouch with our heads pulled between our knees. I'm glad the siren didn't send us scurrying to the basement.

Out on the streets of the village the adults talk about the war. It frightens me to hear all the things that could happen.

So, I'm glad when the war is over. However, the rationing and shortages don't disappear immediately. It seems like a long time before the area alerts and the watch towers that observed the airplane flight patterns become a thing of the past.

General Ike soon becomes our next president. Everyone except Daddy is wearing an "I Like Ike" button.

"Are you a Democrat or Republican?" I hear people ask Daddy.

"I'm neither," he replies. There's a dead quietness as Daddy stretches himself to the top of his short stature. "I'm an Amish man!" he declares. Then a hot debate follows and I run off to play.

Papa's Rope-Making Machine

I step out the back door and lean against the corner post of the porch. Daddy comes out of the garage with a sawhorse, sets it in front of the open door, and enters the garage again. I jump across Mom's flower bed and skip across the lawn to the garage.

"What ya doing, Daddy?" I ask as he comes out of the garage with a heavy cardboard box. He sets it beside the sawhorse. I pull the flap back and see pieces of the rope-making machine.

"Oh! Goodie!" I exclaim and jump with glee. "We're going to make a rope! Can I help?"

"Yes," Daddy says as he picks up the main crank and fastens it to the sawhorse. "I'm going to need all the hands I can get. This is going to be a long, heavy rope."

"What's it for?" I ask.

"Wait and see," Daddy says. I turn and run to the house.

"Come! Come!" I holler as I rush in the back door. "Daddy is going to make a big fat long rope!" By the time Daddy has everything set up many of the neighborhood kids have also gathered to watch and help.

Daddy ties the end of the binder twine to the little turntable with a handle on it and then stretches it down the long lane, placing it into many little hands until he comes to Mom. She's holding the threader. He hooks the twine into the correct notch, then turns back up toward the crank. Back and forth, back and forth he goes. When our hands are filled with the strands of twine, Daddy steps to the crank. A surge of excitement runs through my body when I hear the steady crank of the handle and feel the shreds of twine twisting together in my hands.

"Annie," Daddy calls without losing a turn on the crank, "hold your strings further apart." I do, but then my arms begin to tire again.

"Annie! Be careful! Pay attention!" Mom says as she looks my way. "You can't be gawking around!" I tilt my head toward my shoulder and wipe away a few tears.

The crank becomes harder and harder to turn. Finally, Daddy locks the crank and walks to the end of the rope and takes the threader from Mom. He slowly begins walking the threader up the long binder twine strands that have been twisted together. Behind him a large tight rope drops to the ground.

"Whoa!" I say and shake my hands when the rope eats up the strands I've been hanging onto. I can hardly believe my eyes.

"Daddy, what's the rope for?" I repeat my question several times as I follow him up the line toward the garage.

"You'll see," Daddy says as he lassos the heavy rope around his shoulders. We follow him to the tall old apple tree beyond the barn at the edge of our property. Daddy's flat hay wagon is parked under the tree with a ladder leaning against the trunk. Up, up, up Daddy goes, until he reaches a straight long bough. He fastens both ends of the new rope securely; its loop hangs several feet from the ground. Daddy gracefully scampers down the ladder like a squirrel, picks up a wide board with a "V" notched out of both ends, and places it into the loop of the rope.

"It's a swing!" several voices yell in unison.

"May I ride?"

"May I ride?"

"Be patient!" Mom says. "Daddy has to move the hay wagon first." Many hot summer days are spent breezing through the air under the shade of the tall old apple tree as we push and pump each other on the swing which we helped create.

Epilogue:

After Daddy was diagnosed with Alzheimer's he was living with my youngest son, John, and I at the Children's Home on the edge of the Okefenokee Swamp near Waycross, Georgia. My sister Sarah, now called Sally, brought Daddy's rope machine on one of her visits. Daddy had the boys from the children's home lined up across the yards holding strands of binder twine while he desperately tried, with my help, to recall the steps in rope making. Even so, he and his boys soon had fat binder twine ropes strung across our porches like guardrails!

The Joy of Gardening

Daddy is in the garden walking behind his shiny new red tiller. It is spitting out finely ground soft, moist soil. I am standing on the drive that separates our lawn from the garden that runs from the road to the barn on our four-acre property. I'm fascinated by Daddy's new tiller.

It's spring time! Gardening time! The two have always gone together as far back as I can remember. On the farm I see myself standing at the edge of the flat field across the lane by the large brick house. I am watching Daddy and his big team of horses plow up a section for Mom's garden. He lets it sit a day or two and then runs a harrow over it to break up the clots before smoothing it with a disc. After Daddy sells his horses, I stand at the edge of the same field and watch his Allis-Chalmers tractor turn the soil, harrow, then disc it. That is much faster and easier. Now Daddy's new little garden tractor out-performs both of the older methods.

"Annie," Mom calls, "come, hold this stake." I bounce over to the edge of the garden and grab the stake she's holding.

"Hold it with both hands," Mom says. "Hold it straight!" Mom begins to pound the stake into the ground with a heavy stone. The stake has yards and yards of heavy yellow string wrapped around it with another stake tied at its end. I don't like holding the stake. Every time the stone comes down I fear Mom will miss it and hit my hands. I don't like the vibration that goes up my arms with each thud of the rock.

"Come," Mom says. She picks up the other stake and unwraps the string as I follow her across the freshly-tilled soil to the other end of the garden. Mom stretches the string tight.

"Keep the stake straight and the string tight," Mom says as she pounds the second stake deep into the ground. "What will people think if our rows aren't straight?"

"Annie," Mom says as she rolls the stone aside, "run to the back porch and get the pea seeds." The soft cool moist soil feels wonderful under my bare feet as I skip lightly across it. I fetch the large bag of peas and we drop the seeds into the narrow ditches Mom makes along the stretched string.

"Come here," Mom says after we've planted many rows of peas. She dips her hand into the almost empty bag. "Here are some seeds for each of you to plant in your gardens." I scamper merrily to the top edge of the garden where small sections of soil are roped off for us. I return to Mom for more seed. I want my garden to have lots of peas. Daddy loves peas and I want to surprise him.

After the pea harvest is over and Daddy and I have eaten all the peas, my garden is sadly barren compared to the other little plots lined up alongside of mine. I'm sad, but each year I plant more peas for my Daddy.

DADDY TILLING THE GARDEN

Hits and Misses

Moses builds a huge dog house—much taller than me—for our German Shepherd dogs. It stands against the barn with the entrance facing the road. One day, as I clamber up the barnyard fence and scramble onto the roof of the dog house, I see Daddy come out the back door of the house and head for his big flatbed truck parked in the wide graveled parking area. He's traded his 1940 Chevy for the logging truck and an old Model T Ford. I know he's headed for the woods back on the farm. He cuts young trees and sells them as pallets at the local sawmill.

"Daddy! Daddy!" I call as I slide down the roof and jump to the ground. "Can I go with you?" Several of the others are already on the back of the truck.

"Go ask your mother," Daddy says. I turn and run toward the house.

"Mom! Mom!" I call as the back door slams behind me. I find her mending at the treadle sewing machine.

"Yes," Mom says before I even get a chance to ask. I turn and let the back door slam behind me again as I leap off the porch and head for the truck. The two large German Shepherd dogs are standing nearby with their tails wagging and long tongues hanging in anxious glee.

Soon the wind is whipping loose strands of hair round and round my face as I watch the dogs run with ease beside the truck. I wonder at their endurance. How can they run and never tire? I also wonder how Mom knows what I'm going to ask before I ask. Daddy slows down and waits for an oncoming car before turning into the entrance of the sawmill, but one dog doesn't wait.

"No!" I scream as I hear the screech of tires, a short yelp, and a heavy thud. I hide my face in my apron and cry.

Soon afterward the other dog also gets hit. I don't enjoy going with Daddy to the woods anymore, but I continue to clamber up the side of the doghouse to sit on its roof. It makes me feel close to the dogs again. I like to feel the wind blowing across my face and pretend that I'm sitting on the back of a large workhorse.

One day, as I am enjoying the solitude of the dog house roof, I hear and feel the whiz of a bullet buzz past the side of my head. I hear no shot, neither do I hear it land in the empty lot next door or hit the side of the neighbor's barn beyond. I am stunned.

"God certainly was watching over you," Mom says when I tell her about it. I think of it often, and feel amazed that God knows about me. It is a long time before I am brave enough to crawl back onto the roof of the doghouse.

Epilogue:

I've often thought of this incident throughout the years and am always reminded that my life is in God's hands. His tender, loving care continues to thrill my soul.

The Joy of Singing

"Does your Mom always sing?" a little neighbor boy lisps as he tugs at my arm and looks up into my face. My mind twirls back over the happy years on the farm. Whenever Mom's hands were busy her heart was always singing—while washing dishes, making beds, sweeping floors, kneading dough or washing and hanging out the weekly laundry and then dampening and ironing each piece she's hung. She sang while she and Daddy milked the cows, separated the milk and washed the large milk cans and buckets. She sang while she rinsed down the milk house, worked in the harvest fields or hoed in the garden. She sang as we walked through the woods or rode in the car. Sometimes we sang along with her.

The only time Mom stops singing, it seems to me, is to correct, scold or solve the problems of her six children.

After we move to the village and join the Mennonite Church we attend the mid-winter Bible School. I love the music course Daddy and I attend. We learn to read notes and harmonize our voices. We sing and sing.

Then Daddy goes trucking and the heart for music drops out of my life. Every time Daddy comes home he sings with us.

"Please! Please, Daddy! Please don't leave us again!" But sadly, the day comes when his new orders arrive and he crawls back into the big old cab and drives down the road and out of my life. I weep.

My heart cannot sing for many days. I miss the little bits of wisdom that drop from my Daddy's heart. I miss his jolly voice singing along with the rest of us. I miss the Sunday afternoons in the kitchen when he pops the family's corn. But most of all, I miss sitting beside Daddy and singing, and so I cry and cry. Gradually the song in my heart returns and I begin to sing, and Daddy eventually comes home, only to break my heart afresh.

DADDY - SUMMER, 1951

Epilogue:

After I graduated from High School, Daddy moved our family to Nappanee, Indiana. I went off to college and Daddy quit trucking, but Mom and Daddy got a divorce. During that time there was no song in my heart—no, not until the day God saved my soul when I was twenty-six years old. This new song is a song that rings in the depths of my heart, and no circumstances, even the tragic death of my husband, have been able to diminish or erase it!

Fire!

In my sleep I hear a commotion. Excited voices and scurrying feet awaken me as my brother and sisters crowd around the bedroom window. A strange glow is in the room. I jump out of bed and scurry to the window.

"What is it? What is it?" I ask. No one answers. They're all pressing into the window, so I elbow my way in.

"What is it? Why is everything red?" Flames are leaping high into the night sky from behind the nearest mountain range.

"Why is fire leaping into the sky?" Slowly I begin to realize the flames are coming from the direction of our farm. The whole night sky is lit and spewing billowy clouds of smoke.

"It's our barn!" Mom says sadly as she comes into the room. "Daddy and I are going to the farm."

"Can we come?" we ask as we turn in unison from the window.

"No." Mom says, "It's too dangerous. You must go back to bed." Back to bed! How can I sleep? Are the calves who live in the barn and the new litter of German Shepherd puppies in danger? I press my face against the window pane. The leaping flames, the eerie glow in the sky, and the knowledge of the animals who live in the barn press on my heart. With a loud wail I burst into tears.

"It doesn't help to cry!" Sarah, my older sister, says sadly.

"Dumb!" my little brother replies.

"Go to bed!" Lydie says. I climb into bed, pull the covers up over my head and close my eyes. But I still see flames leaping into the glowing night sky. That horrible red glow won't go away.

I crawl out of bed, press my tear-stained face into the cool window pane, and let silent tears stream down my face. The tightness in my chest increases, so I crawl back into bed, pull the covers over my head, close my eyes and sob myself asleep. I don't awake when the folks return.

"Wake up," Mom calls in the morning as she walks into our bedroom. "Hurry, get dressed. We're going to the farm!" I tumble out of bed, dress, then stumble down the stairs for a cup of warm milk. The others are already crawling onto the back of the logging truck. As we head for the farm, I keep my eyes on the tall column of white smoke still rising into the forest sky.

Even though it is very early, many folks have already gathered on the farm. They stand around in clusters, shaking their heads and talking. I look at the small white columns of smoke and watch them combining into one large thick cloud as they arise from the mound of rubble of what used to be our barn.

Our next-door neighbors have come in an old-fashioned open air Coupe. The trunk is opened into a seat. Many of the men and teenage boys are clustered around the car, examining it while others mull around the barn ruins discussing the cause of the fire. The homeless animals look on in a dazed fashion.

"The fire started from the generator in the milk house," I hear someone say. Now Mom's cousin who has been running the farm for Daddy will have to find other work. Daddy eventually sells the farm and that chapter of my life closes forever.

But for me the burning of the barn doesn't die with the cold ashes. Every night I dream that it is our house that is burning. The fire starts in the closet at the foot of the stairs. Each night the fire grows bigger and I have to decide what to save. I choose a pair of my brother's blue jeans which I'm permitted to wear under my dress for sliding and snow play. Each night I find it harder to go to sleep until finally, in my dreams, our house has burned to the ground also.

Rags and Rugs

I sit in the corner of our raspberry patch and watch a bulldozer scoop a large hole in the ground across the road. The Otto kids are sitting across the fence from me. They're watching too. As the hole grows larger and deeper, mountains of little hills appear around it. A new brick house is being built beside Frances and Philip's lane for Mable. Mable is Melda Otto's mother. I've never seen a house built before, so I'm intrigued.

"You kids stay away," a workman warns. "Big equipment is dangerous!" That's why we stay on our side of the road. When evening comes and the workmen go home we swarm around the hole and slide down the banks of the newly made hills. Every day the bank hills become steeper and that means more fun!

By fall a little brick house is standing on top of the hole. Soon Mable moves in. I like Mable. She's a large, pleasant woman with her thin gray hair pulled into a tiny bun smack on top of her head. She tells us about her childhood.

"I can understand Pennsylvania Dutch," Mable says to Mom one day, "but I can't talk it."

"I've never heard of such a thing!" I say to Mom on the way home. "How can you understand Pennsylvania Dutch but not talk it?"

"I don't know," Mom says. "It's just the way it is." I think about it a lot. It puzzles me.

Mable spends her days making colorful round rag rugs. She tears old clothing into strips and sews them together on her treadle sewing machine.

"Can I help?" I ask as I stand and watch her sew.

"Yes," she says. "You can wind the strips into a ball." I sit on the floor and draw a heap of strips into my lap.

"Wind it tighter," Mable says. I look at the loose ball in my hand, unwind it and start over.

"Here," Mable says, "let me start it for you." I gladly hand over my limp ball. Before long I'm winding a tight ball that passes her inspection. Some of the colorful balls are big, some small and some in-between. I'm glad Mable lets me help.

The next time I come to Mable's house she's sitting in her large rocker, rocking. Three large balls of colorful rags lay in her lap and on the floor. Her fingers fly swiftly as she aptly braids a strand from each ball into a beautiful firm braid. I watch in awe. The braid grows longer and longer as the balls grow smaller and smaller. Soon a heap of braid is piling up on the floor.

"Oh!" I exclaim as I rush into her house the next day after school. Mable is sitting in her rocker stitching the long heap of braid together. She has started in the center of the rug and I see it grow larger right before my eyes.

"Old useless rags are turning into beautiful rugs!" I exclaim. Mable grins and keeps on stitching. I like being with Mable. I ask many questions as I watch the process of rags being converted into solid useful rugs! Best of all, she lets me help and doesn't think I ask too many questions—at least she never says so.

When fall comes, Mable hires my brother Lester to carry two buckets of coal up from the basement every evening. He sets one by her heating stove in the living room and the other by the kitchen range. She pays him twenty-five cents a week. That's a lot of money! Lester is fast becoming rich. I quit worrying about what would happen to us if something happened to Mom and Dad. I'm sure Lester can take care of us.

MABEL AND HER RUG

Epilogue:

As a child I wondered how my neighbor Mable could understand the German dialect but not speak it. Today, after not speaking Dutch for many years, my tongue refuses to cooperate. It feels thick and clumsy when I try. Now I understand Mable's predicament, but I keep working on it!

Changing Lifestyles

The Amish preachers are driving out of our lane. My brother, sisters and I are jumping up and down on the front porch with glee.

"Yippee!" I yell. "We aren't Amish anymore! Now I can play with the English kids in school! Yippee!"

"Didn't I tell you, kid?" Frances asks as she hustles into the yard. "Didn't I tell you it was going to happen? I saw the evidence on your mother's wash line!"

"You see everything," Mom says as she steps out on the front porch.

"Well, you didn't do a very good job hiding it!" Frances retaliates. They both laugh.

The church difficulty started a long time ago. My folks had trouble keeping all the rules. For example, my oldest brother was taking an electronic course, my Daddy's new black Sunday hat's rim was too narrow, and Mom's new ruffled curtains didn't fit in properly either.

I remember the day the ruffled curtains came. Mom had somehow ordered the wrong ones.

"You're going to have to take those ruffles off," Daddy says when Mom puts them up to see what they look like on the windows.

"Oooh, they're s-o-o-o pretty!" a chorus of voices ring out.

"The light shines right through them," I exclaim as I reach out and pull the softness to my cheek. "I like the ruffles!"

"I'm going to have to pick them off," Mom says sadly, "but I'll leave them on for a few days." The days pass and the ruffles remain. Then the day of visitation arrives and my folks share with the Amish preachers their intent of joining the local Mennonite Church.

That summer Mom busily remodels our Amish clothes. When fall comes I walk proudly to school in my transformed dress—shortened, long sleeves cut off and tie-backs and hair ribbons added to match. Best of all, I'm wearing a brand new pair of colored anklets instead of brown stockings.

"How surprised the kids will be when they see I'm not Amish!" I exclaim. But alas, to them I'm still different, so I continue to play ball on the Amish team. My distress increases when my assigned seat is in front of Mark Tressler. He is the class clown and a mischievous preacher's kid. His large family lives on the Mason-Dixon Line with a Maryland address, but near Springs. Mark is full of pranks. He tugs at my pigtails and dips the ends into his inkwell. I don't talk to him or anyone else except two girls that are very kind to me.

Epilogue:

Fifty years later I met Mark Tressler when the town of Salisbury was celebrating the 50th Anniversary of their new high school.

Our class had been the first graduating class. Mark, having a Maryland address, didn't follow the rest of us to the Salisbury. He graduated from high school in Grantsville, Maryland. He had followed in his papa's footprints and had become a preacher. I confronted him about dipping a bashful little Amish girl's pigtails into his ink well. He acknowledged it with a chuckle, and so, my first conversation with Mark Tressler, the tormentor, was a pleasant one.

Roses Are Red

"Mom! Come look!" I call as I turn away from the window in the dining room. "What's going on at Mable's house?" A truck is backed up to the front door, and men are carrying in boxes and odd pieces of furniture.

"Oh," Mom says, "Pearl, Mable's sister, is coming to live with her."

"Where will she sleep?" I ask. "Mable only has one bed."

"Pearl is going to live in the attic room," Mom answers.

"Can I go see her?"

"Yes," Mom says, "but wait until she gets settled."

I soon discover that Pearl's fingers are always busy like her sister's. Pearl does not braid beautiful rugs but creates colorful roses from crepe paper. She is also a lot like our neighbor Frances, who is always busy and running wherever she goes.

"Come up to my room," Pearl says to me every time I visit Mable. "I want to show you my new rose." The little long narrow attic in Mable's house has been transformed into a crepe paper rose garden. Roses of all shapes, sizes and colors hang from the rafters, stand in drinking tumblers and lay in clusters everywhere.

"Oh!" I exclaim as I reach for a big beautiful red rose. "I like this one! It's gorgeous! Will you teach me how to make roses?" Pearl chuckles.

"I want to make pretty roses like you do!"

"Sure," Pearl says. Her face is beaming. However, Pearl soon discovers something I've known all my life. "You're all thumbs and no fingers!" she declares after many unsuccessful attempts. I feel badly. I've wasted a lot of her crepe paper. The paper roses refuse to bloom for me, so I continue to fuss over and enjoy the ones Pearl brings to life. My favorites, of course, are the large red roses. I love them, but what I love more is the glow on Pearl's face when I enjoy the beauty and perfection of the roses she has created.

Champion Worry-Wart

It is fall. Sarah and her Sunday School class are joining the church. During the past summer my folks left the Beachy Amish Church and joined the Mennonites' church. It is in the same village where we now live. Mom is making Sarah a brand new dress and I am standing by the treadle sewing machine and watching her guide the smooth soft material under the pressure foot.

"Please, Mom," I beg. "Please make me a new dress too."

"No," Mom says. "This is a special dress. Sarah is joining the church. When it's your turn to join the church I will make you one too." We are still wearing our made-over Amish clothes. I hate them.

"I want to join church," I say.

"No, you're too young. You need to wait until next year. Then your whole Sunday School class will join after you've gone through the catechisms classes."

"That's just it," I whine. "I don't want to go to the classes by myself. I don't know anyone. I'm afraid to go alone. I want to go with Sarah. Please, Mom, please let me go with Sarah." Tears run down my face.

"OK, OK," Mom finally says. "If it's that bad you may go with Sarah to her weekly classes." I dry my tears. Soon Mom is working on two dresses instead of one. I am happy. I can hardly wait.

"Girls," Mom says. "If it rains you cannot wear your new dresses." Sarah and I are standing in front of the large mirror in Mom's bedroom with our new dresses on.

"Why not?" I ask as I twirl around and look at Mom in astonishment.

"Water will make spots on the material," Mom says.

"Oh no!" I exclaim. Now I have something new to worry about!

"Oh, Mom!" I wail every time I see her, "I hope it won't rain!"

When the special Sunday arrives I am happy to see the sun shining. I'm all smiles; joy is bubbling in my heart.

The girl candidates sit on the front bench on the women's side of the church and the boys sit on the men's side. I carefully smooth my new dress down around my knees and listen carefully. Then the whole congregation drops to their knees. After a long prayer the congregation rises, but we stay on our knees for baptism. I peek sideways through my fingers and see Deacon Yoder pick up the big ceramic pitcher of water out of its large bowl. He walks over to where the boys are kneeling and pours a few ounces into the cupped hands of the Minster. They're resting on top of the first boy's head. A few droplets of water run down the side of his face.

I know I am in trouble. What if some water falls on my new dress? It will be spotted forever!

I am the last one to receive the ritual of baptism. I feel no water running down my face, but what if some droplets dripped on my shoulders?

We stay on our knees while the Minister prays again. Then he takes each boy by the right hand, raises him to his feet, and kisses him. Then the minister's wife pins coverings on the girls' heads before she gives us the right hand of fellowship and a kiss.

But I'm worried. I can hardly tolerate the suspense. Has water dropped on my dress? Has the minister's wife pinned my new covering on straight? All through the morning message I wonder what I look like.

This is to have been my salvation experience. I'll let you judge whether that day I had been truly born into God's family, or if I had been, instead, "A CHAMPION WORRY-WART!"

Bartering Barrettes

My Mom's brother Enos is my favorite uncle. He is the only one who lives in Pennsylviana and he's full of fun. While he laughs and visits with Mom I climb into his lap and run my hands through his light brown hair. He divides his hair down the middle and combs the sides back behind his ears. The bottom of his hair rests on his neck a short distance above his light blue shirt collar. Uncle Enos' sparkling blue eyes match the shirt he's wearing today.

"Annie," Mom scolds, "stop messing up Enos' hair. Let him alone."

"No, no," Uncle Enos says, "we're doing OK."

"Annie, don't talk so much!" Mom says several times.

"Never tell my Annie not to talk," Uncle Enos defends me again. "I've put a lot of time and money into this girl!" His merry eyes dance at me from under his rather thick eyebrows. I cuddle deeper into his arms.

Uncle Enos patiently teaches me to pronounce words distinctly and without a whim. He helps me with German words too. "Bush" (woods) is the hardest of all. For conquering it I receive a quarter, but most of the words are nickel or dime words.

The next time Uncle Enos comes I crawl onto his lap with a comb and a new pair of hair barrettes that I've purchased for ten cents with money I've earned from him.

"Annie," Mom says. There's sharpness in her voice. "Let Uncle Enos alone. You're too big to be getting into his lap."

"Annie will never be too big," Uncle Enos says. He gives me a hug and then examines and "oohs" and "aahs" over my new purchase. "I bet they'd look awful nice in my hair," he says. I comb and fuss with his hair until I am satisfied with the effect of the beautiful little barrettes nestled in his thick hair.

"Oh," Uncle Enos exclaims when I bring him a mirror. "That is so-o-o pretty! I'm going to have to show my family!" He leaves that day with my new barrettes in his hair, and I am holding a twenty-five cent piece in my hand. "When you buy and sell," Uncle Enos says, "you always need to make a profit."

Epilogue:

"Come here, Annie," Uncle Enos says as he gets up and walks toward his bedroom. It's twenty-some years later, and I am the mother of five children. My husband and I are attending the Mast Family Reunion held in Uncle Enos' home in Leon, Iowa.

I follow Uncle Enos. He opens a tiny drawer on the top of his dresser and pulls out the little hair barrettes I had placed in his hair when I was a child.

"Oh," I exclaimed. "You kept them!"

"Of course, I kept them!" Uncle Enos' eyes twinkled with mischief. "I've got a lot of money invested in these little things," he teased. "They've been safe in this drawer. Everywhere we have moved they've come with us."

"Can I have them back?" I asked.

"Well, now," Uncle Enos stroked the thinning hair on his chin. "I don't know. I've got a lot of money invested in them."

"Please?" I cock my head and wait expectantly.

"Well, maybe," Uncle Enos pauses a bit, "if you're willing to pay a dollar." I run to my husband and fetch a dollar, and so, the little barrettes came back into my possession. I carried them fondly home to northern Indiana and deposited them into my little cedar chest that sits on top of my dresser. But I've not been a faithful custodian. Somewhere, somehow, down through the years they've disappeared out of that little chest.

A Pungent Unidentified Odor

Daddy is not logging anymore. He has a job in a garage in West Salisbury. Daddy's boss and his wife are old and very rich. Whenever we visit their large roomy brick home the men usually go to the garage to talk business while the women and children stay in the house. I silently inspect the thick carpets, beautiful drapes, fancy lights and the machine that keeps everything clean. I can't keep from staring at all the fancy stuff.

One Sunday afternoon when we drop by their house another woman is doing something to the boss's wife's hair. She's dividing the hair into little bunches and wetting them with something from a bottle. Then she rolls the little bunch tightly against her head. It's a long, slow process, and there's a strong foul odor in the house.

"Pew!" I say as I grab my nose and lean into Mom's lap.

"Get up, Annie!" Mom says as she elbows me away. I tire of holding my nose, so I whine. The others are making a fuss too.

"You kids go outside and play," Mom says. I'm glad to romp on the thick lustrous lawn. It's a lot better than being in the house.

"Annie," Mom says on the way home. "I'm ashamed of the fuss you made in the house. Those ladies will think I haven't taught you anything!" Then Mom lectures to us about the importance of keeping ourselves clean and taking our weekly baths.

"I don't understand," Mom says to Daddy. "Her house is always neat, clean and sweet-smelling. She herself is a clean person. I have never smelled such a stink in her house before. It must have been coming from her friend, but she didn't look dirty or unkempt, either." Mom has a puzzled look on her face.

"Children," Mom says as she turns toward the back seat, "Let this be a lesson to you. Never skip your weekly bath. You will stink even though you put on fresh, nice-looking clean clothes!" And so it is, every time we pass that way, I think about the lady that doesn't keep herself clean and resolve afresh never to skip my weekly bath.

Epilogue:

After a number of years had passed I was a sophomore in the nursing program at Goshen College. One evening as I returned to the large dorm I was greeted with the same strong distasteful smell from my childhood.

"Oh, no!" I gasped. "Someone is not keeping themselves clean!" I followed the odor and was led to a room full of girls giving each other Toni Hair Permanents. I chuckled all the way back to my room, and I've chuckled down through the years every time it's come to my mind.

I'm *Goverish*

"Annie, you're being *goverish* (indecent). Sit up, hold still, and pull your dress down!" Mom speaks to me with sternness. "What will people think?" We're in Verna's back yard. My youngest sister Erla and I are tussling. Mom and Verna are sitting on the back porch in comfortable chairs having a good neighborly chat. Verna is the grandma neighbor that lives across the empty lot from us. She wears older style dresses and a full apron made of a different print. Her heavy brown stockings are rolled down to the top of her high heeled shoes and her silver graying hair is pulled back into a tight bun.

Ever since I've been a little child Mom has been reminding me to be more ladylike and not to be *goverish.* I never hear her accusing my younger sister Lydie of being *goverish.* Everyone says she's a perfect little lady. I glance at her. She's sitting contentedly on the edge of the porch listening to the women talk. Her legs are dangling properly as she gives them an occasional swing.

"Come on, Annie, play with me!" says Erla as she jumps onto my back. We roll and giggle in the fresh sweet June grass.

"Annie!" Mom's sharp call pierces my joy. I quickly sit up and pull my dress down over my knees.

"Come on, Annie, let's play!" My youngest sister, Erla, doesn't understand.

"Now Barbara," Verna says to Mom in her gentle, quiet way, "let them play. They will only be children once. Besides, they're covered well. The feed bag britches you make for your girls come to their knees. There's nothing exposed. They aren't being indecent. Besides, Barbara, I like watching them. It makes me wish I was young again."

I glance at Mom. She nods an "OK." Erla and I roll in the luscious green grass under the bright blue sky. I hear Verna and Mom laughing. A love for Verna that will last forever springs into my heart.

Taught to Tithe

Every payday Daddy sits at the tall floor-to-ceiling desk and counts his money. The bills that need to be paid are laid out before him, but first he sets aside the tithe. That's ten percent. He puts the tithe into a long narrow leather pouch, folds it in half, and places it into one of the little drawers on the left side of his desk.

On Sunday morning the first one ready for church gets the privilege of dumping the little pouch and dividing the coins into five equal piles.

"I need to brush my teeth!" I exclaim as I pound impatiently on the bathroom door.

"I'm brushing mine," a muffled voice answers. I rush back into the bedroom. My oldest sister is still sitting at the little homemade vanity, combing her hair.

"I'm next," I say as I stand behind her, twisting and turning. "I want to divide the Sunday School money!" The bathroom door opens and I hear my sister going down the stairs.

"I wanted to divide the money," I whine. "I never get to do it."

"Well," Sarah says, "if you'd get up when Mom calls you might get a turn."

"It's not fair," I say as I rush into the bathroom.

When I come down the stairs the large desktop is opened with several stacks of coins standing in a neat row. I pick up one and tie it into the corner of my hankie, grab my coat and Bible, and dash with the others down the tall porch steps to hurry toward the little white wooden church across the road from the store.

"How much should I put into the Sunday School offering?" I ask as we skip along.

"Don't ask me," Sarah says. "That's up to you."

"Well, I want to put some into the big polished wooden platter that is passed around in church too."

"Suit yourself," Sarah says. I wonder why Sarah is always impatient with me.

Our Sunday School class is in a cool little dim room down in the basement. It has only one small narrow window. We keep our coats on. I drop the pennies into the Sunday school bag and keep the bigger change for the church platter.

When we file upstairs one of the girls takes off her coat. She's wearing a beautiful new dress. I keep my coat on. My dresses are all hand-me-downs from my older sister. I wish Mom would make me a new dress and then I'd take my coat off too.

I like to hear the rich deep alto voices of my classmates. I can only sing soprano. When I try to imitate them it somehow doesn't sound right.

One day the deacons visit Mom and Dad. Our church is planning to build a new brick building. Our two pastors are brothers; their family owns the brick kiln. The deacons are asking the church members to pledge how much they can give.

"You kids go out and play," Daddy says. "We've got business to talk about." I'm always glad to be dismissed from whatever I'm doing, but tonight I want to stick around and listen.

"Annie, you go too," Mom says. I shuffle slowly out the back door and flop into Mom's old rocker.

RED BRICK CHURCH – SPRINGS, 1954

Epilogue:

I enjoyed the large warm brick church for several years. Then we moved to Nappanee, Indiana. A few years later my fiancé brought me back to Springs for a visit. The first thing I showed him was the beautiful new brick church. A little sparrow was trapped inside. We captured him at the pulpit and released him outside.

Fifty years later I had the opportunity to worship with a new generation of Springs folks. A large fellowship hall had been added and the parking lot paved and enlarged. Inside it seemed unchanged, except an organ stood in one corner. The organ music blended sweetly with the soft congregational singing and the quiet stillness of the sanctuary. I had the privilege of witnessing the baptism of four teens. They gave their testimonies, then knelt before the congregation to be baptized. A communion service followed.

Mother Learns to Drive

During World War II all the available women go into the factories to replace the men who've gone off to war. They learn to drive cars and function in areas which before have only been proper for men.

"I want to learn to drive the car," Mom says to Daddy.

"There is no need. The war is over," Daddy replies. "There is plenty of gasoline again. I'll take you wherever you need to go."

"Other women are driving," Mom replies. "Why can't I?"

Daddy eventually loses the argument and begins to teach Mom how to drive the old Model T Ford.

"Can I go? Can I go?" a chorus of voices rings out as we cluster around Daddy every time he takes Mom on a driving session.

"No!" Daddy says emphatically. "It is not safe!" He grins at Mom. "Wait until she masters the technique of shifting." We stand at the edge of the yard and watch Mom drive slowly down the lane and onto the road. The old Model T swerves slightly in an unsteady line, then shutters and groans as Mom shifts gears.

"Come on, kids," Daddy says one day. "Mom's doing pretty good!" We pile excitedly into the back seat. When we come to the first intersection, Mom fumbles as she shifts into a lower gear and the old Model T shutters with a series of vibrations. Daddy puts on an exaggerated shaking show in the front seat with his head flopping fiercely. Someone giggles and the rest of us burst out laughing.

"Stop that!" Mom yells at Daddy. "You know it's not that bad!" When Mom is mad her shifting gets worse. She scolds us too—she doesn't like the giggling in the back seat, either.

It isn't long until Mom masters the technique and our fun comes to an end. In 1950 Daddy buys Mom a brand new four-door light blue Ford with large windows. It has an automatic transmission. No shuddering! No fun!

Playing with Paper Dolls

"Let's play with the paper dolls," I say.

"I'm too old to play with dolls," Lydie says.

"Come on," Erla says to Lydie, "play with us." Erla and I run up the stairs to our bedroom, and Lydie reluctantly follows. We each have a family of dolls cut out of the catalog. Each doll is pasted on a cardboard back so that it will stand up.

"Lock the door," Lydie says. Our bedroom consists of two paths: a short one running between the two large metal beds and the other going from our door around the tall old wooden dresser to the closet. Behind the closet door are two decorated crates standing on end. They're several feet apart with a board across them. A ruffled feed bag curtain hangs across the front to the floor and a mirror hangs on the wall above it. That's where we comb our hair.

I'm twenty months older than Lydie. I love to play with paper dolls and I love it best when Lydie and Sarah join us. Then we have a grand old time! Of course, the best time to play is when Mom gets company because we get a break from work.

"Come on, Lydie," I say to her one day. She's sitting on a straight-backed chair in the living room listening to Mom and several neighbor ladies talk. "Come play dolls with us."

"No," Lydie says. "I don't want to play."

"Come on," there's an impatient whine in my voice. "It's no fun if you don't play."

"No," Lydie replies, "I want to visit."

"Come on, Lydie! " Erla says as she comes down the stairs. "Annie won't play unless you do."

"Well, OK," Lydie says as she gets up from her chair and moves slowly toward the staircase.

"My! My!" I hear one of the ladies exclaim, "Lydie is very mature for her age!" After Lydie gets behind locked doors our fun begins.

"Girls!" Mom's voice floats up the stairs and creeps under the crack of our door. We ignore it. Mom's visitors have all gone home.

"Girls!" Mom's voice is a bit sharper this time. "Come help put supper on the table." Quickly our doll families disappear between the mattresses of our beds, and we rush down the stairs to set the table and run errands for Mom.

Epilogue:

Years later my two younger sisters and I were watching our own little girls play with dolls.

"I used to love playing with paper dolls when I was a girl!" Lydie said. My mouth dropped open.

"But," I stammered, "we could hardly get you to play with us. I felt I couldn't play unless you did, because if you were too old, I was older."

"We had to beg and beg before you'd play, and now you say you loved it!" Erla said.

"That was only a front to impress the adults," Lydie said. "I was always afraid that you'd give up begging before I'd give in!"

An Aspiring Author

"Sarah, how do you spell __?" I slap the dictionary shut in disgust.

"Look it up!" Sarah snaps back.

"I can't find it," I tell her as I try to hold back threatening tears.

"That's not my problem!" Sarah says as she gets up and leaves the room.

I don't know exactly when I became conscious of my desire to express myself through writing. It seems as if it has been forever. I'm not able to communicate well, nor can I get the whine out of my voice, but I'm free while writing—that is, if I can find the word I want and get it spelled properly. Even a good dictionary cannot help me, since I do not hear nor pronounce certain sounds clearly. So I ask my older sister Sarah; she's smart.

"I'm not a walking dictionary!" Sarah snaps back at me. "If you want to know, look it up!" I don't know why I bother to ask Sarah, but I do.

I head for the old branchy apple tree up in the pasture on the edge of the field where the gradual upward slope of our property begins its descent into the large forest beyond. The tree is my haven of escape. I sit in its branches and daydream. There's a hollow spot in the crotch of the fork where the two main limbs spring out of the trunk. It contains my secret treasures—just a little bit of this and a little bit of that! But they are treasures, nevertheless, which need concealing from the congestion of our crowded bedroom.

"Listen to this," Mom says one day while she's reading *The Youth Christian Companion.* (That's our Church paper.) "Short Story Writing Contest open for all Intermediate children, ages nine to twelve."

"Can I? Can I?" I bounce up and down in front of Mom's rocker.

"I don't care," Mom says. I run to my tree and begin daydreaming of winning the contest. As I sit in the fork of the old apple tree a plot evolves. A girl my age would hide the family's greatest treasure, the Bible, deep in the hollow of an old apple tree. She would cover it thickly with loose compost, bark and twigs where the searching priests would not find it.

I drive everyone crazy. I need constant help with the proper spelling of words. I search the dictionary but end up crying in frustration. No one wants to help me.

"I'm not a walking dictionary," Sarah says. "Look it up!"

"I've tried, but I can't find the word I want."

"Then want another word!" Sarah says. "If you'd pronounce your words properly you could find them." Sarah leaves the room and I start to cry. Finally, after much frustration and many tears, I walk my sealed story to the post office and drop it into the proper slot. A long wait begins, but when the reply comes, I smile for days.

"Yippee!" I yell and run through the house. "My story has been accepted!" I shout the glad news to everyone I meet. My story is printed in the Honorable Mention section of the church paper that fall! But I suspect they did a lot of proofreading for their young, unseasoned new author.

My Compassionate Friends

It is a hot dry summer. Mom allows us to drag out blankets and sleep on the front porch. One morning when I awake, a little black and white dog is curled up, sleeping at my feet. I throw the covers back for the others to see.

"Look! A little doggie!" I exclaim and grab him into my arms.

"Mom! Mom! May I keep him?" I ask as my head and several others bob up and down excitedly on the front porch when Mom comes to investigate the commotion.

"Please? Please? Mom, may we keep him?"

"Please, Mom, he likes us!"

"We'll see," Mom says. We soon discover that we have not adopted him, but he has adopted us. I love the little dog. He becomes an advocate between us kids and Mom. He objects very strongly when she whips us.

He and my cat become buddies. They do not demand perfection from me, nor do they think I do dumb stuff. They accept me as I am. When I'm down in the dumps I head for the old apple tree up in the pasture. I climb up into the large fork of the old trunk, while the cat scampers higher and the dog chooses a comfortable old hog wallow on the ground. It doesn't take long for my spirits to revive. Sitting in that old apple tree with faithful friends sticking with me is all the therapy I need.

One day I spot several long sturdy sticks lying near the tree. Sliding down out of the fork, I place one stick across a deep hog wallow and jump on it until it breaks. Soon all the sticks are broken into short lengths. Then I run to the front porch and join in the neighborhood board game that's in process. Of course, both my friends, the dog and the cat, follow me.

"Who broke the long sticks I had at the apple tree?" Mom asks as she comes out on the front porch. One look at Mom tells me I'm in trouble. Her arms are propped on her hips and a sturdy whip hangs from one hand. Her beige cotton stockings are rolled down to her brown tie shoes. All eyes turn toward me. Fear grips my heart.

Mom grabs me by the arm and the process begins. Round and round we go with Mom whipping and me yelping. Suddenly, a warning growl erupts from deep inside the throat of the little stray dog. He bares his teeth and flies into Mom. I escape. After that Mom never whips us in his presence. Soon afterward, my little friend mysteriously disappears. He came in the night, and he left in the night. I grieve deeply. My cat tries to comfort me, but I feel very lonely for a long time.

Epilogue:

I do not remember the name we gave that little stray dog, but I do remember the compassion he and I shared with each other.

I Love Company

Four-year-old Perry's eyes enlarge with amazement. He presses his right ear and then his left against the old upright floor radio. We giggle. Perry pushes, grunts and shoves until the radio inches away from the wall. He wedges his head into the gap.

"Where is he?" he asks. "Where is the little man?" He stands looking at the radio with his mouth gaping open. "I hear him, but I don't see him!" We bend over with laughter.

"I haven't had so much fun in a long time!" I say as I collapse on the floor.

"Come, Perry," my older sister, Sarah, says. "I'll help you look for him." But the little man cannot be found. I roll with laughter and pound my fists on the floor.

"There is no little man," Sarah explains to Perry. "It's just the man's voice that we hear through the radio."

Many of Mom's uncles, cousins and brothers travel though the western part of Pennsylvania on their way to Lancaster to visit our host of relatives there. They stop for a night or two at our house. I love it.

"OK," Mom says, "I'm going visiting with Uncle Noah. You girls can have the rest of the day off!"

"Yippee," I yell as I pull off my apron and rush from the kitchen to frolic loose and free.

"Come," Mom says in the evening when she and our relatives return. "Help me strip the beds and put on clean sheets!" We don't mind giving up our beds. We get to roll up in blankets on the living room floor. It's the closest thing to camping out without camping out—especially if there are young cousins on the floor with us. Then we giggle and laugh into the night.

"That's enough noise in the living room!" some gruff, sleepy voice calls down the stairs. I hold still, turn over on my side, and fall asleep.

It doesn't matter if there are no young'uns to play with. Mom's fun-loving brothers and old uncles do a superb job entertaining us. They're full of stories and pranks. They'll pull out their false teeth or a glass eye or do other strange thing.

The Dieners also visit us from my Daddy's side of the family. Most of these cousins are a generation older than me, so I play with their children. I like it especially when Henry's family comes. He's my oldest cousin. They have a girl named Anna Louise, and she's my age. They set up a big tent in the back yard. In the daytime it's our playhouse. At night it becomes a girls' bedchamber while Cousin Henry, his wife and their younger children occupy our room upstairs.

Room for One More

As you approach the village of Springs the road curves around a large plateau of fields. Another curve brings you to the village itself where a dirt road joins the main road. In its fork sits a little round gas station known as the Round House. Men gather around its stove in the wintertime or sit on stumps and crates around its door in the summer. They "chew the cud" and tease the children that come by. When a new block station replaces the Round House it is moved across the dirt road into the pasture by the barn where, for a short time, it becomes the meeting place of the neighborhood kids.

Mark Otto, the second generation owner, and his wife, Dixie, live in a small portion of the large three-story brick home built on the outside curve of the paved road. There is always room for one more in Dixie's tiny kitchen/dining/living room combination with its narrow path surrounding the table.

I love to visit Dixie. She's always cooking, baking or ironing clothes. She sets the ironing board up in the narrow pathway. When she bakes cookies, she carries them to the library table in the entryway to cool.

"Help yourself," Dixie says to whoever is in her tiny crowded space. I love Dixie. It doesn't matter that her eyes are always red and tired looking. She's always kind, soft-spoken and pleasant.

"Annie," Dixie says as she mixes a bowl of cookie dough. "Will you please help Jimmy color, and then read a story to the children?" I love Patty, Marsha, Jimmy, Beverly and David—they're soft, tender and cuddly when they snuggle up close.

On cold wintry days I stay with the children while Dixie washes the family's clothes in the unheated basement. Like the rest of us in Springs, she uses an old-fashioned wringer washing machine that is run by a motor, and then she hangs the clothes in the yard to dry.

"May I bring the children out and help?" I ask on bright shiny winter days.

"They can come out for a little while," Dixie says, "if you dress them warmly." I bundle them into their snowsuits and herd them out the large glass front door, down the broad brick porch steps and out into the fresh sunshine. The children chatter merrily as they help by handing pieces of wash to their mother and me.

"Annie, you'd better take them inside," Dixie says when the basket is empty. I'm glad, 'cause my fingers are frozen. After unbundling the children we cuddle up on the couch and read another book. During the next several days Dixie irons every piece she has washed. I help by doing easy things like pillowcases, tea towels and handkerchiefs.

Dixie is a high school teacher, but she has taken a leave of absence to raise her family. She loves to read and encourages her children, as well as any child who wonders into her small quarters, to read.

"Oh! Lori!" I exclaim one summer morning when I walk into Dixie's small apartment. "You're back!" Lori is Dixie's niece. We hug. Lorie lives in Pittsburgh. That's a big city. She comes to Dixie's house for several weeks each summer. She and I run happily though the forest together. Lorie has never played in a forest before, and I have never had a friend of my own.

Epilogue:

Years later I returned to Springs while attending my thirty-fifth, then fiftieth high school class reunions. I found Dixie dwelling in that large rambling brick home alone with all the rooms available to her. There were shelves and shelves and shelves of books. Everywhere books! Books everywhere!

Her children and grandchildren live in nearby towns and cities. They tenderly surround her with love. How ironic! When she needed space she didn't have it, and now she has it, but doesn't need it.

An Old Pump Organ

"Please? Please? Mom! Please? Please let me take piano lessons! I want to learn to play the piano like Mary Louise does! I want to go to the music teacher's house!"

"No, Annie," Mom says, "lessons cost twenty-five cents an hour. We don't have extra money to spare."

"Please, Mom? Please?" I soon discover begging and moaning does not produce the weekly quarter I need for the hour-long lessons.

Every time I pass the general store I see its large beautiful house set in a green luscious yard with water running in an open concrete duct at its edge. That's where the piano teacher lives. That's where other girls go to learn to play the piano, but not me. My folks can't afford it. Every time I think about it, I feel an ugly pout come from deep within and creep across my face.

I hear girls talk about the beautiful thick carpet on the floor and wonder what it would feel like under my feet. I get excited at the thought of having the teacher speak directly to me or touch my hands as she teaches me to play the piano. I try to get a glimpse of her as I slowly walk past or linger on the railing above the conduit. I seldom see her. I guess she's busy teaching some other girl how to play the piano.

When I am in the fifth grade I learn to read notes and play the tonette. In the sixth grade the class plays the flute. It's fun harmonizing together and my desire to play the piano increases.

"Please, Mom," I beg and cry, "please let me take piano lessons!"

"Annie, stop crying," Mom says. "I said, NO!"

Then one day when I come home from school an old-fashioned pump organ is standing against the dining room wall.

"Daddy! Daddy!" I shriek, "Where did you get it?"

"I bought it at an estate sale in upper Springs," Daddy says. "It was only ten dollars."

"You spoil that child," Mom says. I barely hear what Mom is saying; my joy and the noise I am making on that old pump organ fade out Mom's voice. I tape the names of the notes onto the keys and slowly teach myself to play, but best of all, there are pre-played songs and hymns on scrolls that I can pump out of that wonderful old organ.

Epilogue:

As an adult my desire to play the piano continued. After I had already had several children someone gave us an old upright piano. In the midst of crying babies, diapers and bottles I began to harmonize the base notes with the alto and soprano in certain keys.

When my own little girls began taking piano lessons they weren't twenty-five cents an hour anymore, but I learned many things right along with them. The boys of the household complained of all the noise my singing girls and the piano were making, but I rather enjoyed it.

I'm Glad I'm Short

"Why am I so short?" I ask Mom while we're shelling peas on the back porch. Mom's sitting in her rocker with her lap heaped full of peas. She can shell peas faster then the rest of us put together. Sarah is pretty fast too. She's sitting on a chair near Mom while the rest of us are sitting on the edge of the porch dangling our legs into the flower bed. It's rather hard to balance my container on my lap and swing my legs at the same time.

"Annie!" Mom says. "Hold still or you'll spill your peas!" My swinging legs come to a sudden halt, but before I'm conscious of it, they're swinging again.

"Annie!" Mom says, "Come sit on the floor beside me!"

I get up slowly and move to where Mom is pointing. I'm not comfortable, but soon I forget about it as the emerald green peas keep popping out of their shells into my little tin bowl with a "ting."

"Why am I so short?" I ask Mom, looking up into her face. "I'm the shortest one in my class."

"You're not done growing yet," Mom says.

"Everyone else in school is taller then me, and they're still growing too. It seems as if I'm getting shorter and shorter."

"You're a Diener," Mom says, "that's the way Dieners are."

"But Moses—he's tall!"

"He takes after my side of the family," Mom says.

"Why can't I take after your side?"

"That's up to God, not me! Now, be quiet and shell your peas!"

"Oh! Goodie!" I exclaim when I see the Baker family drive in. "Can we play hide-and-go-seek?" Clifford is my age, but he's tall and lanky.

"You'll have to wait until after dark," Mom says. "These peas need shelling." With astonishing speed the peas pop out of their shells into our bowls, and soon we are free to join in a neighborhood game of hide-n-seek.

"Ouch!" There's a whoop and a holler as Clifford's tall lanky body smacks the ground followed by a groan. Kids come running from every direction. Poor Clifford has been thrown to the ground by Mom's wash line. I watch Clifford slowly sit up and rub his neck with one hand and the back of his head with the other.

Clifford wears a red mark on his neck for a long time. I feel bad, but for once, I'm content to be a short Diener. There are not as many hang-ups!

DIENER FAMILY 1952
Back Row: SARAH (*showing early signs of physical afflications*), MOM: BARBARA MAST DIENER, DAD: ANDY DIENER, LESTER
Front Row: LYDIE, ERLA, ANNIE

Physical Afflictions

Sarah awakes one morning when she is thirteen with her head slightly twisted to the right and dropped toward her shoulder.

"Lift up your head, Sarah," Mom says at the breakfast table after we've prayed. "I can't," Sarah replies.

"Yes, you can. Lift your head!"

"I can't!" Sarah says again. Sarah is known for her stubbornness, so Mom pushes away from the table and fetches the stick. She whips Sarah.

"Now, lift your head!" Mom demands.

"I can't," Sarah says. Mom whips her again. To the day of her death, Mom has never forgotten, nor forgiven, herself for whipping Sarah that morning.

Mom takes Sarah to the doctor. He places her into an upper body cast. When it is removed months later her head falls to her shoulder again. Rounds of tests and hospital stays in far away cities begin. Nothing helps. Sarah's stubborn attitude carries her through life in spite of her severely twisted, uncooperative body that only becomes worse and worse. She is the only one in our family who completes college and earns a bachelor's degree.

Shortly after Sarah's affliction begins, my youngest sister, Erla, develops rheumatic fever. She is in bed long months and develops a serious heart problem.

Epilogue:

My oldest and youngest sisters are not the only ones afflicted. As a young adult, my sister Lydie developed sugar diabetes. We used to say, "Sally has dystonia, Erla has heart problems, Lydia has diabetes, and Anna has babies!"

Tippy, Our New Puppy

Daddy begins a new job in Maryland. Each evening we meet him on Route 40 near Grantsville, Maryland. Our village is only a mile from the Mason-Dixon Line.

"My mama hangs our clothes on the Mason-Dixon Line," Mark Tressler, a boy in my class, says every time Mason-Dixon Line is discussed in school. The Line runs through their farm. I'd like to go see it, but Mom says it's just an imaginary line.

Daddy's work crew is always late. One hot muggy evening while we are waiting a dog with a litter of pups comes around the corner of the garage. They are all black, but one has white paws, a white tip on its tail, a bow on its neck and a white spot on its forehead that runs down its nose. Mom and several other ladies are sitting on old rickety wooden chairs in the shade of the garage. Every time I pick up the white-tipped puppy he licks my face and wiggles.

"Can we have this puppy?" I ask Mom as I deposit him into her lap.

"He's cute!" my littlest sister, Erla, says.

"Mom, can we have this puppy?" I repeat my question several times as I jump up and down excitedly. "Please? Can we take him home? Please, Mom?"

"He likes us!" the twins say.

"No!" Mom says. "No more dogs!" But we know that Mom loves animals. So we keep plopping the puppy into her big lap. Every time he jumps out or Mom puts him down, one of us puts him back into her lap and then runs off to play.

TIPPY AS A PUPPY

Daddy is late coming home that evening, and when we drive out onto the highway the little white-tipped puppy is still in Mom's lap.

"We will call him Tippy," Mom says. "When I was a girl we had a little black dog named Tippy. He was marked somewhat like this puppy. I wrapped him in a blanket, rocked and sang to him until he fell asleep." In the back seat I wiggle and squirm with excitement. I can hardly contain my joy.

The next day Mom begins her training program for Tippy.

"No! No!" I cry and grab the puppy when I see Mom coming with a rolled up newspaper.

"Put that puppy down!" Mom says sternly. "Don't interfere, or I'll whip you too!" I learn quickly not to meddle with Mom's "Institution of Correction." Every time I hear the crack of the newspaper I wince and cover my ears while Tippy yelps and runs around the side of the house. Mom goes the other way. They meet head on. Tippy yelps and flees again. I cringe, but it isn't long until all Mom has to say is, "Tippy," in a stern voice, and he immediately responds. She teaches him to never leave our four acres unless invited to go along.

We Learn to Share

While I am growing up there is very little that I can call my own. We share most everything. There is one bedroom and closet for us four girls and one bedroom for the boys. There is one bat, one jump rope, one wagon, one bicycle, one dog, two sets of skates, but whole litters of kittens and bunnies.

The younger ones use the wagon and the older ones, the bicycle. Being a middle child I have little chance at either. Of course, our baby sister has her own private tricycle.

"Come," I call to my younger brother and sisters as I rush into the house. "Sarah is going to ride the bicycle. She's pushing it into the pasture!" There's a rush of feet and the slam of the back door as we jump off the porch and head for the hillside by the barn. Sarah reaches the top of the slope, turns the bike around, throws one leg over the tall top bar and then settles herself on the seat. Lester gives Sarah a running push and she pulls her leg up off the ground. We cheer! Down the hill she rolls, faster and faster. When the bicycle begins to fall, Sarah leaps across the handlebars. We laugh until we, too, drop to the ground.

"Stop laughing," Sarah snaps at us with fiery eyes as she pushes the bike up the hill for another try. She soon masters the skill of balancing and rides all over the village with ease. Then, whenever I find the bicycle unoccupied, it is my turn to learn.

"Scaredy cat," my brother says. "You're too scared to let me push you."

"Go away," I say. "I don't want you to push me."

"Scaredy cat! Sissy!" he says. I wipe moisture out of my eyes. He's right. I'm not brave like my sister, and I'm not going to let him push me. So it is a long time before Mom says I'm steady enough to ride on the paved road that runs though the village.

"Mom, can I ride the bike to upper Springs?" I ask one lazy hot summer day.

"If you think you can manage all the curves coming down," Mom says.

I hop on the bike and ride to the store, then push the bike up the steep curvy hillside. I'm excited as I turn our bike around and throw my leg over the bar. As I push off I crouch forward. The wind rushes past my face. My pigtails sail out behind as the bike flies smoothly around the descending curves. But, alas, the bottom of the hill approaches too soon.

"My turn," Lester says as he reaches for the bike. I sit on the cool shaded store porch, swing my legs and wait for another turn.

"Let's walk around The Horn," Lydie says. It's another lazy summer afternoon. We've gathered on the back porch, sipping tall glasses of Kool-Aid. "The Horn" is the little dirt road that leaves our village at one end and wanders around down by the river bottom, then turns and comes up at the other end of our village.

"I'll take the bicycle," Sarah says.

"That's not fair," I say.

"Annie, quit your fussing," Mom says, "or, you're not going."

"We'll take turns," Lester says. So off rides Sarah on the bicycle. We see her turn off at the little dirt road by the schoolhouse. We follow. Soon we come to the edge of the forest. The bicycle is lying in the ditch.

"It's my turn," I say. I hop on and peddle off. Soon I catch up with Sarah. I ride past, drop the bike in the ditch and begin walking with her. When the other group reaches the bike that I've dropped, someone else rides ahead, drops the bike and joins Sarah and me. I feel blessed that we have a bicycle to share. We each get several turns on the bike before the road comes up out of the valley and meanders on up toward the other end of our village. No one, not even Lester, is strong enough to ride all the way up that hill.

Kitty Face—Me?

I step out onto the back porch. Mickey Mouse, my gray and white cat, wraps herself around my legs. I feel the vibration of her gentle purr. With one quick swipe I stoop down, gather her into my arms and bury my face in her soft fluffy warmth as she continues to purr.

"Annie!" Mom's sharp voice startles me. "Put that cat down and get in here." I drop Mickey Mouse, brush myself off and slowly return to my pan of scalded peaches.

"Wash your hands!" Mom says. "You were holding a cat!"

"Kitty Face!" my brother Lester says as he makes a face at me. I wipe away a few tears as I step to the sink, rinse my hands and then return to my chair. We're canning peaches and the kitchen is stuffy hot, but the loose peelings slip off quickly. I drop my skinned peach into my sister's container. When Mom gives us a break I return to the back porch. Mickey Mouse is waiting for me.

"Kitty Face!" my brother says as he slips past me on his way to the basketball hoop mounted above the garage doors of the barn. I cuddle Mickey Mouse closer. I don't mind when adults say my round smooth face reminds them of a cat. They say my laughing wrinkles dance beside my eyes like cat whiskers. But I don't want my brother to tease me, so I stick my tongue out at him.

"Annie," Mom says. "Be nice. How do you expect to go to Heaven if you're not nice?"

"Kitty Face!" Lester calls over his shoulder. I lift my shoulder and wipe my eyes.

"You're my best friend," I whisper into Mickey's ear. "You never scoff or make fun of me. You're always your faithful furrypurry self." I cuddle her close while she purrs her unconditional love into my life, and sunshine breaks into my soul again.

Epilogue:

Yes, I had a friend like everyone else, only my animal friend never betrayed me like friends who are people do. However, I betrayed her when I left her to move with my family to Indiana. She ran away from the home I had placed her in, and I have not seen Mickey Mouse since. Neither have I forgotten her.

The Dreaded Time of Butchering

Raising our own food including our meat is a normal part of farm life. The butchering season in the fall is a fun time for me, that is, until Mom decides I'm old enough to help with the gruesome process. Then it becomes a time of drudgery.

When we moved into the little village of Springs we brought along two cows, two hogs and the hens. So, fall butchering continues to be an annual process. I hate it!

A severe crisis comes into my life when Mom decides to raise and sell butchered broilers instead of laying hens in the large chicken house on the second floor of the barn. Mom buys hundreds of day-old rooster chicks. She nurtures them in the little brooder house in the field beside the barn. It's on skids so Daddy can move it around.

"Come," Mom says to us when it's time to move the young roosters to the large henhouse above the garage. We do it after dark. Mom snatches the sleeping roosters by the legs and hands them to us two at a time. I try to stay in the shadows.

"Here, Annie," Mom says, handing me two roosters. "Where have you been?"

"Right here," I say as I timidly take the roosters by their legs.

"Well, you use more energy trying to stay out of work then it takes to pitch in and do it!" I lift my arm and wipe the tears out of my eyes. I hope the young rascals won't give my legs a good flopping with their wings before I reach the large hen house. Some do, some don't.

Several months later the roosters are ready to sell. Mom has many orders. People want to buy her freshly butchered roosters, so every night after school my free time is spent plucking sticky feathers and pulling out yucky guts after my brother Lester chops the heads off. Mom scalds the roosters in boiling water to loosen the feathers. My sisters and I sit in the grass and pluck and pluck and pluck those yucky feathers. Yuck! Yuck! Yuck!

"Annie," Mom scolds. "Don't just sit there. Pluck them feathers."

"How can I?" I whine. "These yucky feathers are sticking to my fingers."

"Shake your hands," Mom replies. But shaking doesn't help much, so I wipe them on the grass before I plunge in for another handful.

"Here," Mom says, "give me that chicken. You take this one. Pull everything out of its insides." I flop the plucked chicken on its back on the plank that is stretched out between two sawhorses. I prefer using these sawhorses for rope-making rather then this! Slowly I insert my hand into the opening that Mom has cut between its legs. It is warm and moist. I grab a handful of "innards" and pull. The intestines come and come.

"Get the gizzard and liver too," Mom instructs. How can Mom see everything?

Tears fill my eyes. I wipe my face on my upper sleeve and keep pulling.

"Can I go?," I ask when the last of the day's quota is met.

"Yes," Mom replies, "but stay close by. You'll need to set the table soon." I skip off, but the remaining live roosters in the large second floor of the henhouse stand as a heavy shadow over me, and they will until the last rooster is plucked and sold.

Every time the large chicken house is emptied we spend several nights scooping out the old litter and scattering it evenly across the garden and raspberry patch. Then we sprinkle a fresh coat of sawdust on the floor and the process begins again.

I used to enjoy Mom's fluffy yellow baby chicks, but not anymore. Every time we empty the brooder house she fills it up again. I sigh. I know that the beautiful little chicks are headed for the dreadful butchering block that I desperately despise.

I'm glad for the short reprieve from butchering, but I wonder why Mom isn't content with the money she makes from the hundred-pound bags of popcorn she buys from a local farmer and resells in the village. We peddle it for her. Now, that's fun!

Recognizing Evil Impulses

"Annie," Mom says. "Go to the garage and fetch me a hammer." The screen door slams behind me as I jump off the edge of the back porch and run across the lawn. The large barn/garage/chicken house combination is located beyond the wide graveled drive that surrounds our house and yard. The garage is on the right. A winter's supply of hay is stacked to the ceiling along the back wall. Daddy has a workbench on the adjoining wall. The tools hang neatly on a pegged board above it on the other side of the window. The board is painted white, and beneath each tool is painted its actual shape in bright green, like the trim of our house. Woe is us, for Daddy can tell at a glance what tool is missing.

I reach up and remove the hammer from its position on the pegged board. With my finger I trace the perfectly shaped pattern painted beneath it. I turn and walk past the brand new light blue Ford Daddy purchased for Mom. Suddenly a strong impulse to smash the new car with the hammer surges through me. I grab the hammer with both hands and run out of the garage.

"What's wrong, Annie?" Mom asks. Without answering, I hand her the hammer, rush up the stairs, throw myself on the bed and cry. I don't know where that frightful impulse came from, but I don't like the way it gripped my heart.

Epilogue:

Years later, my husband and I were driving along a dark country road. A toddler was sitting between us and a baby on my lap. We drove past a house nestled in a large lawn. Framed within a lighted picture window was a man sitting in a recliner reading the paper. I was hit with an impulse to pick up a gun and shoot him. In a flash, Daddy's new car and the hammer incident returned to me.

In shock, I cried out to the LORD to deliver me from the evil impulses of my own heart. As an adult I knew where these impulses came from, for the Bible says, "The heart is evil and desperately wicked…out of the heart proceed evil thoughts, murders." That includes my childish heart as well as my grown-up adult heart.

Wiggling to Get My Way

Daddy is in the field above the barn near the big old apple tree with the tall swing. He's digging large rocks out of the pasture. He's wearing my favorite red plaid shirt, and I think it's his favorite, too, because it's thin and very faded. I hear his sledge hammer crushing into a rock over and over again. Surely there is no daddy as strong as mine. He throws the crushed pieces onto the back of his oversized truckbed. It's big because he used to haul logs out of the forest. I skip up the lane and join him.

ANDY DIENER & NEW CAR - 1957

"You pick up the smaller pieces," Daddy says, "I'll get the big ones." With enthusiasm I sling crushed pieces onto the bed of the truck. But as usual, I tire quickly. I sit in the tall grass and watch, then crawl into the truck and mess with the knobs on the dashboard. I pull levers and I flip switches.

"Daddy," I call, sticking my head out the window, "what is this for?" He comes to the window to see what I'm talking about. I ask him many questions about every gear, knob and lever. Mom says asking questions is the most efficient ability I have. "I want to know about all this funny-looking stuff inside the truck," I say.

"Daddy," I ask after I've disrupted his rock-crushing career half-a-dozen times. "Do you think I know enough to be able to drive the car?"

"Oh, you should," he replies without looking my way as he keeps on crushing rock. I crawl out of the truck, run through the pasture, roll under the fence, cross the broad parking area below the barn, run though the yard and into the house. The screen door bangs behind me.

"Mom! Mom!" I call, "Daddy says I know how to drive the car!"

"I'm not sure about that," Mom says. As usual, she's busy at her treadle sewing machine. She doesn't even look up.

"Daddy taught me," I say. "I really know how! He said I could!" After much begging, Mom finally lays aside her sewing and walks with me to the garage. She backs the brand new 1950 light blue Ford out onto the parking area and slides over to the passenger's side. Our dog Tippy is standing beside me with his tongue hanging out, his tail going fifty miles an hour and a pleading look in his eyes.

I open the back door and he jumps in. Tippy nestles onto the seat behind the driver and sticks his nose against the window. I crawl behind the wheel. Mom shifts the car out of park and slowly I push my foot against the gas peddle. The car moves forward. I push harder. The car is headed for the garden.

"Turn! Turn!" Mom yells. I turn the wheel sharply. Now I'm headed toward the pear tree.

"Stop! Stop!" Mom yells. I slam my foot onto the brake. Mom and I are thrown against the dashboard. I hear a yelp from Tippy as his body is thrust against the back of my seat. I jump out of the car and retrieve him. He hobbles on three legs for several days. After that no one can persuade Tippy to ride in the car. Neither can I persuade Mom that I can drive, that is, not until after I've taken the Driver's Education Course at school.

Moses is Unhappy

While we lived on the farm at the foot of Mount Davis, my oldest brother, Moses, was extremely terrifying to me. I was sure he was going to kill me. After we moved to the little village of Springs there are no longer many places to hide from his wrath, so I was glad when Daddy hired him out to local farmers.

"Annie, you've been in my room!" Moses yells from the top of the stairs. He and Lester share a bedroom. Moses is very smart and electronically minded. He can build or do anything, so Daddy buys him an Electronic Correspondence Course. Now he tears old radios apart and builds new ones. He has mysterious projects in his bedroom with wires and tiny little bits of odd things laying neatly on the windowsills, dresser top and chair. There are larger things stacked in corners. During the week, while Moses is working for the farmer, I often step into his bedroom to look at the strange, neat assortment of things scattered across his dresser top and chair. I don't touch anything.

"It was my turn to clean your room," I answer timidly from the bottom of the stairs. It is hard to speak with fingers of fear griping my chest. "I didn't touch anything."

"Mom," Moses yells. "Keep them kids out of my room!"

Moses is not happy with his farm job. Neither is he happy with his name. The kids at school tease him, make fun of him and call him degrading names. So when he is seventeen he runs away from home and joins the Air Force. I'm happy for the reprieve. He changes his name to William, but we call him Bill.

Decree # 7674

When Moses runs away from home and joins the Air Force I rejoice, but Mom spends several days in bed crying. My sisters and I push our younger brother, Lester, into the corner behind the kitchen door.

"Promise," we say to Lester. "Promise that you won't break Mom's heart by running away and joining the Air Force when you grow up."

"I won't do that," Lester says as he breaks free of our grasp and runs out from behind the door.

Mom slowly recovers from the shock, but then Moses calls again.

"What? What?" Mom speaks loudly into the old crank phone which hangs on the wall of the little stairway platform. We gather around the railing at the bottom of the stairs.

"What? You changed your name? You changed your name to Moses William?" Mom asks. We look at each other in amazement.

"Just plain William! Oh, Moses, what did you do that for? You know you were named after my father! Oh, Moses! What will people think?"

My brother Moses has never cared what people think. So, by Decree No. 7674 during the September Term of 1954, my brother Moses officially becomes William, and Mom spends several days in bed crying. However, Moses changing his name doesn't change his character, even though his torment does become a bit more acceptable.

My sister Sarah loves cooking. She makes good stuff, but she also makes the biggest messes I've ever seen! I know because I have to clean up after her. One summer after she's a teenager, Sarah volunteers to work in the kitchen of the church camp at Laurelville. When we go to visit, everyone is calling her Sally. Again Mom cries. Sarah has been named after Mom's step-mother.

"If you change your name too," Mom says, "what will people think?" However, Sarah is like Moses. She doesn't care what people think.

The next summer Sarah volunteers to work at the camp again. Mom goes into the office with her to make sure she gives her proper name. The rest of us follow quietly behind Mom like a family of ducklings.

"Oh, dear!" the Registrar exclaims, "We already have two Sarahs working in the kitchen! Can we call you by another name?" Sarah looks at Mom.

"Well, I guess," Mom says, a bit slowly, "I guess you can call her Sally!" And Sally she has been ever since!

Epilogue:

As adults, Bill and Sally never got along. He was persistent and she was stubborn. If Bill wanted to make Sally mad, he called her Sarah, using the German pronunciation, and Sally retaliated by calling him Moses. Then the sparks flew.

LYDIE, ERLA , ANNIE (AND TIPPY)

Deception: Rabbit or Chicken?

"Mom! Mom!" My brother, my sisters and I jump up and down. "Please, can we have a rabbit?"

"I want to raise rabbits," I say. We are in a rabbit barn up over the mountains. They have several rooms full of rabbits in cages. I like the cages full of colorful bunnies.

"The bunnies are so-o-o pretty," I say. "Plea-s-e, Mom, can we raise bunnies?"

"I have enough chores," Mom says, "without taking care of rabbits."

"But Mom," I grab her arm and jump in front of her, "I'll take care of them. I will, all by myself!"

"No," Mom says.

"Please?"

"No!" But a short time later we drive down the mountain with two white adult rabbits in our trunk.

Daddy builds pens and nest boxes. Mom purchases heavy feeders, water crocks and a big bag of pellets.

"After you sell your first litter of bunnies," Mom says, "you will be on your own. I will not buy any more feed or supplies for you." The rabbits belong to all of us; however, I become the chief caregiver. I love the rabbits and don't mind the profit being divided equally among us.

In the summer we move the rabbits to grazing pens. In the winter we feed them hay, which we've gathered from along the ditches and stored in the large empty dog house by the stable door—that is, until we run out. Then I snitch hay from the cow's manger.

As our rabbit production increases, I become especially fond of one little bunny. I call him "Typewriter." He is white with two rows of black spots on his back. I refuse to sell him.

"Annie!" Mom says whenever she sees me cuddling him. "Don't make a pet of him. He needs to do his share in this rabbit business too." But he and I have already become buddies, so I protect him from the butcher block. It seems more and more people want their rabbits ready for the stew pan.

"I'm afraid that rabbit is getting too big to sell as a fryer," Mom says one evening when she sees me carrying him in my arm as I do my chores. I sigh a sigh of relief.

That winter the temperature drops and stays below zero for many days. Mom takes care of all the outdoor chores when she goes to milk the cow. I'm thankful for her kindness. When I return to the barn I cannot find Typewriter. I've been keeping him in the farm wagon with the load of hay. It's parked in the garage. I search and call, but he doesn't poke his nose out in response.

"Mom! Mom!" I call as I rush into the house, "I can't find Typewriter. I've looked everywhere! I can't find him!"

"Oh," Mom says calmly. She doesn't look up from the pot of stew she is stirring. "We had him for supper two nights ago!"

"What!" I shriek. "You killed Typewriter? You knew he was special to me!"

"And you knew before we began raising rabbits that they were not for pets but for food," Mom replies calmly.

"You told us we were eating chicken!" I groan and shake with sobs.

"If you had known, you and some of the others would not have eaten the meat." I have no reply. I run up the stairs to our room, throw myself on the bed and cry out my sorrow into my pillow.

Tippy: the Rabbit Dog

While Tippy is still young, Moses, whom we now call Bill, comes home on a leave from the Air Force. He sits on the back step and polishes his gun. Tippy finds a comfortable spot, settles in and chews on the toe of Bill's boot. Bill gets up, takes his gun and the dog and heads for the woods.

"That dumb dog will never amount to anything!" Bill declares when they return. "All he did was chew the toe of my boots!"

"I don't agree with that," Mom says, "He obeys better than the kids. I only speak once to him!" That makes me happy—not that Mom thinks Tippy listens better than us kids, but that, in her opinion, he's become a valuable member of our household.

Our rabbit business is multiplying, so Daddy builds two large grazing cages, which we turn upside down in the yard or garden. I love to see the little bunnies, most of them white, hopping friskily on the bright green grass.

"The bunnies are out!" I yell the next morning. Little white bunnies are hopping here, there and everywhere, and so are we. Tippy joins in the chase.

"Look at Tippy!" Erla yells. I turn around. Tippy is strutting toward us, his head held high, with a bunny held by the nape of the neck. The bunny is swaying back and forth in the rhythm of Tippy's gait.

"Yea! Yea! Yippee!" I dance and twirl as I join the cheer that's going up for Tippy. I rush toward him and throw my arms around his neck. He places the bunny gently into my hands and then bounces off after another one. Lester helps me move the cage to another spot. Soon all the bunnies are safe inside again.

"Yea for Tippy!" I throw my arms around his neck the second time and he licks my face.

The next day I hear a whine and then a scratch at the back door. I go to investigate. Tippy is looking up at me with a wild bunny in his mouth. He has a pleased look on his face. I follow him to the rabbit cage and release his catch into it. Soon he's back with another one. Tippy's prized rabbits don't do well in captivity. They soon die, but Tippy doesn't understand that. He keeps bringing them in.

"Tippy will not meet you after school tonight," Mom says one wintry morning as we file out the front door. "We've had a new litter of bunnies last night. He'll be on bunny duty!" Newborn bunnies bounce like jumping jellybeans. If they bounce out of the nest they fall through the screen to the cold cement floor below. When Mom hears Tippy bark, she hurries to the barn. She finds Tippy under a rabbit cage on the cold cement floor with a hairless bunny between his front legs. His jaw is over the bunny as he barks at the cats who are sitting in a semi circle in front of him waiting for a snack. Mom chases the cats away and replaces the bunny into the warm, cozy fur-lined nest.

"Thank-you, Tippy," Mom says, patting his head and handing him a treat from the house. Tippy is pleased. He gobbles the nugget and runs happy excited circles around Mom's legs.

Exposure to a New Culture

It's Christmas morning. I am excited, but Daddy is jubilant. He has a secret for Mom and he's anxious to share it.

"Please, Daddy?" I beg. "What is in Mom's box? What makes it so heavy?"

"Wait," Daddy says. There's a big smile on his face. I'm happy because Daddy's happy.

Finally, we gather around the gifts. Daddy reads the Christmas story from the large Bible, then we kneel and pray. Daddy thanks God for the gift of salvation that was supplied for us on that first Christmas day. Then, finally, it is time to unwrap our gifts.

"Mom's gift is special," Daddy says, "it'll be the last one opened!" So, after all the other gifts are opened, Daddy reaches under the tree, picks up the heavy, nicely-wrapped shoe box and places it on Mom's lap. I hold my breath as she slowly unwraps it and carefully opens the lid. Inside lay several large rocks! With a startled cry, Mom jumps out of her rocker and the box and rocks roll to the floor while she flees up the stairs to her bedroom. Loud weeping comes floating down the stairs. The room where we are sitting is very quiet. It's not often we hear our mama cry.

Daddy leans over and pulls a little slip of paper from underneath one of the rocks. He slips it into his pocket, then quietly goes up the stairs to Mom. I hear the door close softly behind him.

How could Daddy do such a mean thing? Is my daddy like the man in the true story "Light from Heaven" that Mom reads to us each week from the church paper? That father was cruel. He never gave gifts to his family. One year he wrapped hunks of coal in shoe boxes for them. The little boy and mother wept for days. Now my mama is upstairs weeping.

I hear the upstairs door open quietly and Daddy comes down. He looks sad. Without saying a word he slips out the back door. I watch him disappear into the barn. We are excitedly preparing to try out our two sets of roller skates that we received, but suddenly I want to be with Daddy.

I drop the skates I've been claiming, and follow Daddy to the barn. I find him sitting in the darkened stairway that leads to the chicken house. His head is in his hands with his elbows propped on his knees. I sit down beside him.

"Daddy," I whisper. "What did that little piece of paper say?"

"Well, Annie," Daddy says sadly as he turns his head toward me. "I went down to Frostburg, Maryland, to buy your mother an electric stove. They were out of the style I wanted, so they had to order it. It won't be in until the middle of January, but I paid for it. When I go back to pick up your mother's new stove, all I need to do is show them this little slip of paper, but your mother doesn't believe me. She thinks I'm playing a mean trick on her."

"I believe you," I say as I nestle into his arms. Soon the others come into the barn on their way to the empty concrete chicken floor to roller skate. After a while I follow them and take my turn on the two sets of skates we have received for Christmas. When I check on Daddy again, he's gone.

Epilogue:

Coming from the Amish culture of that day, my mother had many things to learn, but by the time I was an adult she understood more about the ways of modern living then I ever expect to conquer. She was never fooled in such matters again.

Crying for My Daddy

Daddy doesn't like digging ditches for a living. The hours are long and hard and the pay is poor, so each evening he searches the newspapers for a better job. That's when he finds the ad, "Truck Drivers Needed." Daddy reads the ad out loud several times.

"It's a trucking company in New York City," he says to Mom.

"Driving truck is not the right job for you," Mom says. "It'll take you away from home. We need you here."

"I know," Daddy says, "but, I need to take care of my family. I can't find anything around here." Daddy applies and his application is accepted. He needs to go to New York for a week of training.

Mom drives Daddy to the bus station in Somerset. Tears run down my cheeks as we slowly make our way through the mountain valleys and ridges. Then Daddy climbs into a big blue bus and disappears down the highway. I cry all the way home. I cry all night.

"I want my daddy," I sob in the morning.

"Your father has spoiled you rotten," Mom says. I cry all day. I cry until the long week is over and it is time for Daddy to come home. Then I'm excited.

"We're going to go get Daddy," I tell everyone. "He's coming home on a bus." I can barely sit still in the back seat of the car as Mom drives slowly up and down and around the many curves. When we arrive the bus is not there. We wait and wait, but it does not come. When it starts to get dark Mom goes to the window to inquire. I crawl out of the car, stand beside her and grab her apron.

"There is no bus coming from New York until tomorrow morning," the lady says. I cry. My body shakes with sobs as we drive away. We slowly make our way up, down and around the little coves toward home.

"Stop crying, Annie," Mom says every few minutes. "Crying will not bring your father home." But painful sobs and deep disappointment keep crushing my chest while large silent drops roll out of my eyes and dampen my dress.

With laden steps and a drooping heart I slowly plod up the stairs with the others and plop onto the bed without undressing and cry myself to sleep.

I awake! The sun is creeping above the horizon. Somehow I'm under the covers. I hear heavy footsteps on the stairs and I sit up in bed.

"It's Daddy!" I screech and throw the covers back across my sister. In one leap I'm out of bed and into his arms. "Oh, Daddy! Daddy! How did you get home?"

"I walked," he says calmly.

"But the agent said. . ."

"The agent was wrong! My bus came in minutes after you left." Daddy says as he sits down slowly on the top step and removes his shoes and rubs his feet.

"Why didn't you call us?" I ask.

"The telephone exchange was closed for the night," he replies.

"Oh, Daddy! Look at the holes in the bottom of your shoes!" I burst into tears.

"It feels as if the bottoms of my feet have holes too," Daddy says. He reaches down and rubs them. "I walked on the grassy bank most of the way."

Mom comes out of her bedroom. She looks at Daddy's blistered feet and then hurries to bring a pan of hot Epson salt water to soak them. I continue to cry.

As it turns out, Daddy does not get the job in New York City, and I've never been happier!

Daddy Trucks—I Cry

"Daddy, what are you doing?" I ask. He has a newspaper spread out on the dining room table and is leaning over, searching through its pages.

"I'm looking for a better job," he says as he puts an arm around me and draws me close. "I can't be digging ditches all my life. It's hard work and the pay is not enough."

"Please, Daddy! Don't get a job far away like the trucking job in New York."

"Annie, I have to take what I can find," Daddy says. That day a great fear grips my heart every time I see Daddy bent over a newspaper.

A short time later the North American Moving Van Company from Fort Wayne, Indiana, hires Daddy. He's away from home long weeks at a time. I rejoice every time he comes home. It's usually just for a few days and then away he rolls again, but for now, our family is complete.

"Let's sing," I say as I run for the stack of songbooks. I slide in beside Daddy. I love to listen to his mellow voice and hear his adventurous tales. But when the time of his departure draws nigh I drop into a deep despondency.

"Please! Daddy, please don't leave!" I cling to him with a tear-stained face. However, he crawls back into that big old rig and drives out of my life, leaving my heart crushed and broken.

"Annie! Stop crying!" Mom says. But I can't stop crying. Tears are fast becoming the major ingredient in my life! I cry every time I can't have my own way. I cry every time I can't understand something.

"Annie, stop crying," Mom says. "How do you expect to get to Heaven if you're crying all the time?" But the biggest hurt and crush of all is when Daddy crawls into his rig and drives out of my life.

The Challenge of Economizing

After Daddy begins trucking, things at home become economically tight. Unexpected operating expenses are high and uncertain, and Mom never receives a regular amount of money from which to plan a budget. Often she denies herself to supply the needs of her children. We remain basically unaware of Mom's dilemma. Because of her large garden, canning habits and ability to make-do we always have plenty to eat and enough coal for the furnace.

MOM (BARBARA MAST DIENER) & DADDY (ANDY DIENER)
IN HIS NORTH AMERICAN TRUCKING UNIFORM

Mom puts our welfare ahead of her own personal needs. She even gives us each one stick of gum a week. My brother and sisters break their gum in half or chew it in one chunk. I break mine into seven pieces. I hide my pieces in the back of my drawer and chew a piece every day.

"Give me some gum," my littlest sister begs. Reluctantly, I walk into our crowded bedroom and grab the two wooden knobs on my long heavy dresser drawer. My drawer is next to the bottom. I pull it open and dig in the furthest corner where my horde of tiny pieces is hidden under my clothes. When my fingers make contact, I pull out one piece.

"Here," I say as I hold out a daily allotment.

"I don't want a little piece. I want more," Erla says as she brushes my hand away. I reach back under the clothes and retrieve a second piece, then break the remaining pieces in half.

As Daddy's trucking skills increase so do his paychecks. Mom begins giving us an allowance of twenty-five cents a week. The others buy candy, ice cream and gum. I save mine. I want to buy a camera.

"Annie, I need a dime," my brother Lester says. "May I borrow a dime?"

"No," I say, "I'm saving my money to buy a camera."

"I'll pay it back the next time we get our allowance," Lester says. "I'll give you an extra penny to boot!"

"OK," I say and scurry off to fetch Lester a dime.

And so, while the others chew their gum and eat their candy, I save my allowance and buy a camera. Slowly I fill up a shoebox with family pictures. Mom claims the box. She likes my pictures; they make her laugh.

When I am older I become a babysitter. I get twenty-five cents an hour. Then the neighbor across the road opens a pretzel factory in the basement of his house. He hires me in the evening to bag the pretzels at twenty-five cents an hour. I am full of joy—that is, until the pretzel factory has a fire.

Epilogue:

I left my box of pictures with Mom when I entered college. Years later, after I was married, I went to claim my pictures, but they'd been spread out among the family. I guess they got a large share of my allowance after all!

All of the pictures in this book were taken with this camera. I am actually the face behind these pictures.

Fresh Air Children

Each summer the Mennonite Church brings youngsters from New York City to spend several weeks in country homes. We call them "Fresh Air Children." Mom applies for two girls.

"Oh, goodie! Goodie!" I jump up and down with glee when I hear the news, but I'm *really* excited the day Gracie and Candy arrive. Candy adapts readily, but Gracie doesn't like our country ways and is very outspoken about it. She's chubby and hard to please. We favor quiet, gentle, fun-loving Candy.

"Gracie," Mom says, "will you say 'grace' before we eat?"

"No," Gracie snaps back. "We don't pray at our house. We just eat!" We double over with laughter until one of us falls off the bench. Even though I'm laughing, I can't imagine eating without first thanking God for our food.

Our way of eating is very strange to the girls and Gracie eats very little. One day Mom cooks spaghetti in a creamed sauce for dinner. Gracie slouches in her chair and refuses to eat, but Candy eats whatever Mom gives her.

"Gracie, sit up and eat," Mom says.

"My mama's spaghetti is red," Gracie says, "and it has meat in it." My eyes grow big. I've never heard of red spaghetti with meat in it.

"Sit up and eat," Mom commands. "We don't eat like that!"

I ponder the strange ways of Gracie and her family. Even after she's gone I cannot forget her. Then one day I visit the neighbors next door. They are sitting around the table eating sandwiches, laughing and teasing each other. In the middle of the table stands a tall thin bottle filled with something red. One of them reaches for it and douses his sandwich with the red stuff. Some misses and falls onto the table. With one quick swipe of the finger it is plopped into his mouth. Is this what Gracie's mother uses to make her spaghetti red? (I did not know about catsup or casserole cooking until I entered college.)

Troubling Decisions

"I want to be an artist and paint pretty pictures," I say.

"That would be worldly," Mom replies. "Artists and writers are lazy people. They sit around in the mountains and beside lakes and paint pictures and write stories instead of working. People will think that I didn't teach you how to work!"

"I won't be lazy," I say.

"But they aren't good people!" Mom continues darning the hole in my brother Lester's sock. "I want you to be a good person."

"I will be a good person, Mom! I'll work hard." I run and fetch the Sears Roebuck Catalog and leaf through its pages until I come to the large paint set.

"No," Mom says. "I told you that would be worldly!"

"But I want it. I want to paint pretty pictures." I pester Mom for many days.

"Well," Mom finally says, "you can have it for Christmas. But I still don't think that you being a painter or a writer is good." I jump with glee.

My two younger sisters are looking at store-bought dolls in the catalog. We've never had dolls like that. Mom makes us rag dolls. The fancy catalog dolls that my sisters want seem dim in comparison to the beauty of the large paint set.

"Are you sure, Annie," Mom asks while she is preparing the order, "that you don't want a doll instead of paints?"

"No, I want the paint set!" I reply

"Remember, once I send in the order it's too late to change your mind."

It seems like a long time before Christmas morning rolls around. When I see the beautiful, cuddly dolls in my sisters' arms, a flood of tears and self-pity overcomes me.

"I want a doll too," I say. I had no idea how beautiful a store-bought doll would be or how cuddly it would feel in my arms. I had been deceived when I insisted on a paint set. The pictures in the catalog deceived me!

"Annie! Is that the way a Christian should act?" Mom scolds. "You're getting too old to play with dolls anyway. Stop crying! You've made your decision." Even so, a flood of tears comes every time I see my sisters playing with their beautiful dolls. I am enjoying my giant paint set and do not want to give it up, but I cannot take my mind off my sisters and their beautiful dolls.

One snowy February noon I walk downtown during our school lunch break. I'm in Junior High now. I see an exotic soft rubber doll in the drug store window. She is much smaller then my sisters' dolls, but she looks so real and I want her. When I get home I dump my savings on the bed and count, but there's not enough! I walk daily to the drug store to check on the doll in the window.

"I don't have enough money," I say to Daddy the next time he comes home. Tears are running down my face. "I'm afraid she will be sold before I can earn enough."

"Come," Daddy says. "Let's go look at your doll."

"That's a pretty nice doll," Daddy says as he fishes in his pocket for the extra money I need. It is February twelfth, President Lincoln's birthday.

"You spoil that girl rotten!" Mom scolds Daddy when we come home.

"Annie paid for most of it," he says. I call my doll Betty Elizabeth. I search through the Sears Roebuck catalog just like Betty Durst's mom does and design a lovely wardrobe for my new friend. I'm glad Mom lets me use her treadle sewing machine and odd pieces of material.

Epilogue:

I cherished my doll even after my own little girls were playing with their dolls, and even after her soft rubber skin filled with tiny rotten pin holes. My adult children threw my poor Betty Elisabeth away—'cause she was rotted away. But I've kept the many delicate garments I had made as a young girl. That little doll taught me the principles of designing and tailoring clothes for myself, and later for my own children.

Our Sit-Down Strike

"I don't want to pick raspberries," I grumble as I flop to the ground between two long rows. "It's too hot!"

"Well," Mom replies, "what if I'd say I don't want to cook supper because the kitchen is hot?"

"That's different," I say.

"No, it's not," Mom says. "Get up and start picking!" With a face longer than a mule's I get to my feet.

Our large half-acre patch with its thirteen long rows is between the road and the garden. At first Mom pays us a penny for every quart box we pick. That's pretty good! As demand and production increase, so does our pay, but it stabilizes at three cents a box. Mom has many eager customers who come to the house for her berries.

I like picking raspberries. We sing as we pick our way down the long rows, but there is one thing I like better, and that is popping a handful into my mouth.

"Annie," Mom says, "quit eating berries! Put them in the box!"

"I do declare," Mom says on another day, "you pick the most, eat the most and leave the most behind!"

"Oh, Tippy! Tippy! Come here!" I call when I see him coming down the long row toward me. I need a break. Tippy's tail is swaying his chubby body from side to side. He seems to be smiling as he looks into my face. "Come here, Tippy!" I stop picking. I stop singing. I stop eating. I love Tippy, and Tippy loves me! It is his personal responsibility and delight to keep check on each one of us as we slowly move down the long, sun-scorched rows of berries.

"You're the bestest friend ever," I say as I hold out my hand with a few berries in it. His warm moist tongue sends little love thrills into my heart. I throw my arms around his neck and then reach into my box and give him a few more berries. Soon he's off to check on someone else.

Mickey Mouse, my cat, however, spends most of her time with me. She and Tippy are best friends. She winds herself around his legs just like she's doing now to me. She's looking up expectantly at me and purring. I stoop down and give her a pat on the head and a few strokes down her back and up her tall tail. Poor Mickey Mouse, she doesn't eat berries.

One summer the neighborhood buzzes with the news of the C. L. Lewis' "sit-down" coal strike. I can't image grown men refusing to work.

"How can they make more money by not working?" I ask. If they worked for our mom they wouldn't sit down on the job. I know, I've tried it!

"Hey," Lester says one day when the sun is extra hot. "If the coal miners can sit down and refuse to work until they get more pay, why wouldn't it work for us?"

"I don't know," I say slowly. "We'll probably get a whipping."

"Naw," Lester says, "it's the modern thing to do."

"Yippee, let's do it," I say. I'm always ready for action. We each take our partly-filled raspberry box and sit at the entrance of the row we have been assigned.

"Why aren't you picking berries?" Mom asks when she comes to check on us.

"We're on a sit-down strike," Lester says. "We want more money."

"Get up!" Mom says, "Get back to picking! What will the neighbors think if they see you sitting here?" Mom turns and goes back into the house.

"What are you kids doing?" a neighbor lady asks a few minutes later as she walks by.

"We're on a sit-down strike," Lester says. The lady laughs and bustles on down the road. By the time Mom returns to check on us, there is a collection of neighbors in the driveway by the raspberry patch.

"OK," Mom says, "Get back to work. These berries need to be picked!"

"Now, wait a minute, Barbara," Frances says. "These children work hard and they work long. The sun is very hot. Don't you think they deserve a raise?" After a little bit of talking back and forth with the neighbor ladies, Mom gives us a two-cent raise.

"Yippee!" We jump to our feet. "Now we'll get five cents for each box we pick!" No one complains when Mom raises the price of her raspberries a nickel, and we are top news on the neighborhood gossip lines. Our sit-down strike worked just like it did for C. L. Lewis and his coal miners. I feel rich.

Yucky-Tasting Medicine

One summer during raspberry-picking season I break out with a miserable case of the hives. None of Mom's home remedies work, so she takes me to the doctor. He gives me a bottle of brown yucky-looking stuff. The label reads, "Take one teaspoon four times a day!"

"Annie!" Mom calls after we arrive home. "Come to the kitchen and take your medicine." When Mom opens the bottle, a horrible expression crosses her face. She quickly measures out a teaspoonful.

"Oh!" Mom says and turns her head to one side. Then she looks back at me.

"Open your mouth!" I do and almost choke to death! I'm sure it's the stinkiest, most horrible, foulest-tasting stuff to ever hit the market!

"Oh," Mom says after I recover from the coughing fit. "We can't keep this stinky stuff in the house! People will think I'm a bad housekeeper." She marches out the back door onto the porch. I feel numb as I watch her stuff the bottle and a spoon onto a rafter ledge near the ceiling.

"Annie," Mom calls me four hours later, "go to the back porch and take your medicine." I know it doesn't do any good to argue, but I do some quick reasoning. If this stuff is too stinky to keep in the house, then it certainly is too stinky to swallow.

I obediently reach up and take down the bottle and spoon from the ledge, then walk to the edge of the porch. Mom watches from the open doorway. My back is toward her. I unscrew the lid and lay it on the bench where she can see it. Then I pick up the spoon and pretend to pour myself another dose. I tilt back my head and swallow a spoonful of air. I groan, cough, gag and make a horrible face. After awhile Mom trusts me and doesn't supervise my medicine-taking. Then I begin to empty the bottle, one spoonful at a time, into the flower bed and cover it like a cat. Gradually the bottle becomes empty, and amazingly, my hives disappear!

Romping in the Woods!

"Mom! Mom!" I rush into the house. "Mom! Mom!" The other kids are right behind me and Tippy, our dog, is jumping with glee.

"Mom! Mom!" I flop my books and empty sandwich bag on the counter and rush with the others up the stairs to change my clothes. We make ourselves peanut butter and jelly sandwiches and then head for the woods. Tippy, our dog, Mickey Mouse, and several other cats follow.

I'm glad Mom's not home. When she is, she always has jobs for us to do. If we can make it through our little-two acre field and crawl under the fence into the large grazed rock-covered pasture of the forest, we are beyond Mom's voice calling us back.

"Yippee!" I yell as I skip from rock to rock and play a game of tag with my brother and sisters.

"Let's go to Plymouth Rock," I say. It's down near the spring and it's the biggest rock in the woods. It's also nestled in the tallest weeds of the woods. It has foot holes grooved in its side.

"Do you think it was an Indian who chipped the foot holes in the rock?" I ask as I follow the others through weeds much taller than me. No one answers.

"There it is!" I exclaim when I get the first glimpse of Plymouth Rock. We scamper to the top and sit Indian style on its flat surface. Tippy and the cats maneuver around its base.

"I'm going to look for arrow heads," Lester says as he shimmies down the rock and moves slowly through the tall weeds toward a nearby Indian mound. Tippy follows. I hear Lester stomping around, but Tippy doesn't make any noise.

"I'll beat ya to the spring," Lester says as he returns to the Rock. We scamper down and race through the weeds toward the cool, refreshing water that's bubbling out of the ground and trickling down the hillside. I cup my hands for several refreshing sips. Tippy and the cats refresh themselves further downstream.

We lazily maneuver over into an opened section of the forest. The crumbled foundation of an old cabin sits in the cleared area on the crown of the hill by the edge of a fenced field. There are no weeds here. The grazing cattle keep it neat and clean. In the spring hundreds of bright yellow daffodils bloom in the clearing around the old foundation. We sit on the old crumbling stones and survey the newer homestead off in the distance at the foot of the hillside.

Next, we turn back into the forest, climb under a barbed-wire fence and follow the little creek that has sprung from the spring. It soon deepens into a deep gorge. I watch the others walk across the long log thrown across the gorge. That's scary, so I crawl. The cats walk ahead of me with their tails held straight up in the air while Tippy comes behind me with his tail swaying merrily from side to side.

"Come on, Annie!" Lydie calls. "Get up on your feet!"

"Sissy!" Lester says with a chuckle.

"Look! I'm doing it," Erla says. I ignore them and keep crawling. It's scary enough as it is. We visit Alta Schrock's summer cabin and peak in the windows, but we only get a tiny glimpse of the inside. Then it's time to start home. The brier patch we have to go through is the least enjoyable part of the woods for me. I always get several nasty scratches.

I'm glad to see Mom by the time we get home. Supper is on the table waiting for us. Our appetites are in place, and we eat well. I'm glad Mom never scolds us for running off into the woods.

An Accident

One Saturday Uncle Enos drives into our lane with two large stems of bananas for us kids to peddle in the village. After hanging the stems on a rafter in the basement, he cuts off a large group, then divides it into small bunches and gives them to us kids to sell. He pays us well.

After we cover the homes in lower Springs we load our faithful red wagon with more bananas and head up the steep winding hill to upper Springs. The bananas sell well. When our wagon is empty and our purse is full we head home.

"I'm not going to walk down this hill," I say. "We have an empty wagon!" I flop into the wagon with one knee and begin pumping with the other. The others pile on behind. Faster and faster rolls the wagon. We drag our feet. At the steepest point of the descending road, the rubber tire on the left front wheel peels off. The wagon veers off the road and the steel rim cuts a large gaping hunk out of my knee. I'm thrown into the ditch, and I scream as blood squirts from my knee. Lydie takes off running down the hill.

"Come back! Come back!" I screech at the top of my voice. At the first curve she disappears into a house. A few minutes later a car drives up the hill with Lydie in it. The lady puts me in the car and drives me home. The others bring the wagon.

Mom takes me out of the lady's car and places me into our car.

"Stop crying," Mom says. "Crying doesn't help!" But I can't stop crying. When we reach Salisbury, all the doctors' offices are closed. I sit in the car and wail. Finally, Mom finds an eye doctor. He carries me into his office and sets me on a chair, then with a needle and thread begins to pull the large gaping hole in my knee together. I scream!

"Stop making so much racket!" Mom says. "What will people think?" I don't care what people think—it hurts!

"I'm sorry," the doctor says. "I don't have anything to numb it." He calmly continues to pull and sew the large gap in my knee together, and I continue to scream.

When Uncle Enos hears about the accident, he comes to visit. I climb into his lap and jabber on and on and run my finger through his hair. Mom's working at the sink.

"Doesn't this girl ever stop talking?" Uncle Enos asks.

"Annie, be quiet!" Mom says in a stern voice as she turns toward me.

"No! No!" Uncle Enos says as he holds out a hand toward Mom. "Don't ever tell this girl to be quiet. I've got a lot of money invested in her." He reaches into his pocket and gives me a dollar. That's the most he's ever given me. I love Uncle Enos. I throw my arms around his neck.

I hobble my way around Junior High that fall and am not very pleasant to live with.

"Don't touch my knee!" I exclaim and pounce on anyone or anything that gets too close.

"Annie," Mom says, "be nice. How to you expect to get to Heaven when you're such a grouch?" I burst into tears. It seems as if my knee will never be normal again.

Epilogue:

I've entered my retirement years now and my knee has functioned well, although it has remained sensitive.

A Jubilant Show of Joy

Each fall when school opens Tippy is lonely. He knows when the school bus will go past the house. I sit on the driver's side so I can see Tippy in the yard by the edge of the road. No matter what the weather—rain or shine—there is Tippy with his tail wagging fifty miles a minute.

The bus drops us off at the elementary school beyond the house.

"Wait on me," I call to the others as I hop up on the long narrow porch that runs along the front of the little country store. The screen door slams behind me as I rush to the tall stack of cubby hole mail boxes to the right of the door. I stretch on my tippy toes and turn the knob of Box #1. It's in the top left hand corner. I pull out the mail and the screen door slams behind me as I jump off the porch and hurry to catch up with the others. I'm out of breath by the time I do.

Before we reach our yard I see Tippy. It looks like he's turning himself inside out with excitement. His tail is going fifty miles an hour, whacking against one side of his body and then the next. My cat, Mickey Mouse, sits calmly by with her tail curved smoothly around her slender body. She is also waiting for us to come home from school. She's not moving a muscle except the very tip of her tail. It twitches a bit. I think she's telling Tippy to control himself, since there is enough commotion coming down the road.

"Hello, Tippy!" I drop everything in a pile and throw my arms around his neck. I receive a generous sloppy bath of kisses before he dashes off to the next one. After he's greeted us all he picks up a book or a piece of mail and marches ahead of us toward the back door of the house while Mickey Mouse trails on behind. Mom is sitting in her rocker in the middle of the kitchen with a large pan of apples on her lap. We each grab a chair and form a circle around her.

"Here, Tippy," I say as I tap the extra chair I've pulled into the circle. He hops up and sits erect.

"My turn!"

"My turn!" Several hands reach out for the *schnitz*, or 'slice' of apple Mom is peeling. Tippy doesn't say anything, but I hear his tail thumping. He doesn't even notice when his *schnitz* is only an apple peel.

"Annie," Mom says one beautiful warm spring afternoon as she comes to the back door. Tippy, Mickey Mouse and I are on the porch enjoying the warm spring sunshine. "I want you to bathe Tippy." I get up and reach for the round galvanized tub hanging on a nail against the inside wall of the porch. Tip's eyes immediately drop and a pout forms on his face. He circles up tightly on the rocker I've just vacated. I drag the tub into the yard and begin filling it with buckets of warm water. Tippy's large brown eyes watch every move I make. An occasional shiver runs across his body.

"Come, Tippy," I call as I suds up the water. Reluctantly and very slowly he slides out of the rocker and creeps on his belly toward me. I pick him up and "plop" into the sudsy tub he goes. The scrubbing begins. He stands perfectly still. After I've scrubbed him, I shove him into a sitting positing and then on into the water.

"No! No!" I place a hand of restraint on his back every time he attempts to shake himself. When I release him, the "jubilant show of joy" begins—a vigorous shake, a run around the house, a rub down in the sweet green spring grass. Of course, in his exuberance I receive many wet, joyful kisses of thanks.

"Annie," Mom calls from the kitchen door. "Don't forget to clean up the mess!" That statement tarnishes my joy.

The Other Side of the World

"Listen to this," Mom says as she looks up from the *Youth Christian Companion*. She's browsing through our weekly church paper and we're gathered around her rocker waiting for the weekly edition of our favorite story, "Light From Heaven."

"What is it? What is it?" I ask excitedly as I step onto one of her rockers.

"Get off!" Mom says as she elbows me away.

"Read it again," I say. "Read it again!" We crowd in closer.

"Wanted—Pen-Pals for Foreign Children. All ages needed." Mom reads it slowly.

"Can I? Can I?" I bounce up and down and grab the back of the wicker rocker even before Mom finishes reading all the fine print.

"Annie, let loose of my chair and hold still!" Mom reaches up and slaps my hands. My sister Sarah and I are the only ones that qualify. I'm bursting with excitement, but Sarah sits quietly, waiting for me to settle down so Mom can read the additional information.

That evening Sarah and I fill out a form with our names, ages and address. A long wait begins. Then information arrives that our names have been added to a list available to pen-pals in foreign countries around the world. They would choose us. Now a longer wait begins.

I hop off the school bus every day at the elementary building and rush diagonally across the street to the post office. Would I have a letter? Would someone have chosen me?

Weeks pass. I begin to despair of having a foreign pen-pal. I quit stopping at the post office. One day the postmistress hands Sarah a funny-looking envelope. A few days later I receive one. Then two or three arrive every day. Soon it is a handful. Before long the postmistress is handing each of us a big bag full of letters. Sarah's bags are always fuller then mine. She's in the teen category.

"What will people think when they see the bags of letters you bring home?" Mom asks. "They'll think you don't have anything better to do!"

"Oh, Mom!" Sarah says as she dumps her bag onto the dining room table. "This is a pretty good thing to do!"

After Sarah and I eliminate the letters that only consist of requests of things to be sent to them, the task of choosing a pen-pal is much easier.

Gradually the bags full of letters taper off. We both write to several, but we each end up with only one faithful pen-pal apiece. Mine is a girl from Australia, and Sarah's is a boy from Africa.

As my special friend and I write back and forth, I begin to learn some amazing things. While I am sitting in school, she is sleeping. While I am enjoying beautiful summer days, she is building a snowman. While I am celebrating Christmas in the winter, she is celebrating it in the summer. It's hard to conceive of Christmas without snow, and she can't imagine Christmas with snow!

Epilogue:

After I graduated from high school my family moved to Indiana and I began college. My pen-pal and I lost contact with each other. Even though I don't remember her name, I still think of her occasionally and wonder how life has been treating her and her family on the other side of the world.

Witty Uncle Enos

I like it when Mom's uncles and brothers stop to visit 'cause they're plumb full of pranks, jokes, and teasing. Mom's Uncle Dan and his family lived in Pennsylvania a long time before we arrived. Great Uncle Dan is very old, though. He doesn't play with us kids.

Mom's brother Enos followed Uncle Dan to Somerset County then convinced my folks to come. I like Uncle Enos. He's always coming out with pranks, humor and witty sayings. He has a ready reply for anything we kids can throw at him. But no matter how hard we try, we cannot outwit him.

One day we come home and find Mom's false teeth on the windowsill above the kitchen sink with a slice of bread stuck between them.

"Uncle Enos has been here," we chuckle in unison. I run and look behind the kitchen door. The shelves are freshly stocked with loaves of bread for us kids to peddle.

Uncle Enos moved his family to Oklahoma to take care of Grandma and the farm. When he returns to Pennsylvania on business he usually stays at our house. Sometimes his son, Amos, is along. Amos and I are the same age. We have more modern conveniences at our house then they do in theirs. We're Mennonites—they're Beachy Amish. One day, to tease Uncle

Enos, we put up signs to explain our modern conveniences throughout the house.

"Hey," Uncle Enos calls as he comes halfway down the open stairway. "Did you want the water left on in the bathroom sink?" We'd hung a sign "Running Water" above the faucet.

"No, of course not!" several of us reply in unison.

"Hey, Amos," Uncle Enos turns and calls back up the stairs. "Turn the water off. They don't want it running!" We double over with laughter. That's one of the things I like about Uncle Enos—it's impossible to outwit him!

Mom's Sunday Afternoon Nap

It's Sunday afternoon. Mom is in her room taking a nap. We are preparing to go to the woods.

"Let's pop popcorn to take along," I suggest.

"We need to ask Mom," Erla says.

"Annie, you tip-toe into Mom's room and ask," Lydie says.

"No!" I say. "You go! I asked the last time."

"I'm not going," Lydie says.

"OK," Lester says. "I'll go." Lester tiptoes into the room. He slides quietly between the bed and wall until he reaches Mom's pillow.

"Mom," Lester whispers as he leans over and shakes her gently. "Mom, can we pop popcorn?" I hold my breath. Lester stands quietly by the bed until he receives a grunted approval. With a whoop and a holler we frolic down the stairs and into the kitchen.

Lydie grabs the popper off the bottom shelf behind the door. I pull the half-empty five-gallon lard can out from under the kitchen sink and dip a hunk into the popper. Lester carries the large popcorn container over to the stove and turns on the burner. Erla grabs the measuring cup out of the can and with one quick swish dips it full.

"OK," Lester says to Erla when the hot lard begins to bubble, "dump in the corn." I like to hear the sizzle and crackle that follows.

"My turn at the crank," I say as I step up on the stool in front of the stove. I feel very grown up as I take the little red knob from Lester and turn the heating kernels inside the kettle. That is, until they begin to pop very rapidly.

"The lid's sliding off!" I yell. Lester steps up and rescues our corn while the rest of us scurry after the fresh fluffy kernels on the floor. When our bag is full we leave the house, mess and all, and head for the woods.

Mom gets tired of being disturbed during her Sunday afternoon naps, so she devises her own plan. While we are eating dinner she takes a pad of paper, a pencil, some snacks and trinkets, and heads for the woods. She creates a "treasure hunt" that leads us back and forth throughout the woods looking for her hidden nuggets while she's at home taking a nap.

Epilogue:

Years later my house was full of small children and it was my turn to covet a quiet Sunday afternoon nap. The woods my children frolicked in were in northern Indiana, and the only hill, a barn hill, but one fact remained the same. On Sunday afternoons, I'd be awakened by whispering at my door. Then the door would open quietly and one of the older ones would creep up to my bed.

"Yes," I said in a sleepy voice the first time it happened—even before he had chance to ask. "You may pop popcorn."

"How did you know what I was going to ask?"

"Moms have ways of knowing," I mumbled, turned, and pulled the covers up over my head.

Back row from left: SARAH, MOSES & ANNIE
Front fow from left: LESTER, ERLA (WITH DOLL) & LYDIE

Transforming the Chicken Coop

"Annie! Annie!" Mom's strong, shrill voice floats up through the pasture behind the barn. "Annie, come here." My sisters and I are hanging wallpaper in our new playhouse in the small chicken coop near the woods. Mom is not raising broilers any more. She's given the coop to us girls and that makes me very happy. We scrubbed it clean until it passed Mom's inspection, then she gave us the leftover pieces of wallpaper that have collected over the years.

"Annie! Annie!" Mom calls the second time. I enjoy hanging the strips of paper on the wooden walls of our new play domain. It makes me feel grown up doing it without Mom's help. "Annie! Annie!" I drop the rag I'm using to smooth the paper firmly onto the wall and run down the hill to the house.

"I need something from the store," Mom says. "Just hand this note to the clerk." I take the note and run down the road. I'm in a hurry to get back to the chicken coop, so I run all the way. I'm out of breath and breathing heavily by the time I return. Mom points to a chair. I sit. She hands me a tall glass of water. I gulp it down. Then she dismisses me, and I run back up the hill to my sisters.

It takes several days to neatly paper the ceiling, walls, two-by-fours and the little shelves and window sills. We're not as fast as Mom. It's slow work maneuvering the dampened paper into the many cracks, crevices, corners and angles. It takes a lot of patience and a lot of trying again. My sisters and I are pleased with the results, even though our little home is full of many shades, colors and designs.

"You've done well," Mom says when she comes to inspect our finished work. So we set up housekeeping in our decorated chicken coop. It feels cozy. The cats become our children. Lydie's and my cats cooperate. They're old and well trained, but Erla has a young kitten who doesn't think sitting just "so-so" in a child's highchair is great sport. The poor thing gets paddled and scolded again and again. I feel sorry for the kitten. But no matter how hard Erla tries, the kitten doesn't stay put.

"Girls," Mom's voice floats up the hill and around the barn into our newly created Heaven. We ignore it.

"Girls!" Mom calls again. "I need your help!" There's a bit of sharpness in her voice this time. Quickly, we leave our sleeping cats and hurry to the house. The minute we are free again, we slip out the back door and up the hill to our sleeping cats…well, two of the sleeping cats, UNTIL the next time we are called away

Epilogue:

Years later, my husband, my two oldest children and I were visiting in Springs. I spotted the little chicken coop still sitting in the pasture and asked permission to visit it. I was amazed—our wall paper job was still in tact. I marveled at the neat square corners we'd created as we papered each beam. I doubt if I could match its neat perfect performance today.

Canned *Futzhes*

My baby sister, Erla, wants to spend the night with her friend

Patty. Patty lives up across the mountains, but Erla has never been away overnight before.

"You're too young," Bill says. "You'll cry!" He's home on leave from the Air Force. He doesn't hit and kick us any more, but he torments us in other ways.

"No, I won't," Erla snaps back. "I won't cry. Patty and I are friends."

"Oh, yes, you'll cry," Bill says. "You'll miss my *futzhes* (stinkers). You'll need a *futz* to take to bed with you!"

"No, I won't," Erla tilts her chin in the air and slaps Bill. "I won't cry! I don't want your dumb old *futz*." I'm amazed every time I hear my baby sister snapping back at Bill. When I try to talk to him I stutter, get tongue-tied and say dumb things. How can my baby sister be so brave?

"I know what I'll do," Bill says. "I'll put a *futz* in a glass jar for you!"

"No, you won't," Mom says. "What will people think?"

"No," Erla says. "I said I don't want your old *futz*!"

The next day after school Erla happily climbs on the school bus with her friend. They have fun and play contentedly all evening. At bedtime there's a knock on the front door. When the door is opened no one is there, but an empty glass jar is sitting in the door jam. Erla bursts into tears. The family does not know why Erla is crying. They cannot console her, so they call Mom, and she fetches her home.

"See, I told you," Bill says, "you couldn't stay overnight because you'd miss my *futzhes*."

The Maze of High School

I am filled with excitement and fear as I watch the big yellow school bus pull up in front of the large brick four-room elementary school building set in the large playground across the corner from the village store. A shiver runs down my spine as the elementary students file off the bus and us local high school students file on. It's my first day in Junior High at the large brick two-story high school with its large rooms, high ceilings, rows of tall windows and broad central stairway leading to the second floor.

The bells fascinate me. When they ring we file into another room for another subject. The halls get jam-packed with students going every which way. It's hard to keep up with my classmates. I'm afraid of getting lost.

Each homeroom has its own cloak room. I look for an empty hook to hang my sweater, and then stow my lunch sack below it.

"Good morning, Anna," one of my classmates say.

"Uh huh." I grunt my reply, fold my arms tightly across my chest, drop my head and shuffle out of the overcrowded room.

Mr. Showalter is our homeroom teacher. Each morning a student from our class reads a portion from the Bible that's on his desk. Then we stand and salute the flag. However, Earl reads from his Catholic Bible, Sonya from her Jewish, and I always read John chapter three from the Bible I carry with me. I read it fast. Daddy has given me a dollar for memorizing it. He'll give me five if I learn it in German. I try, but I never conquer it.

Our Typing and Shorthand teacher, Mrs. Hillegas, and Mrs. Deal, our English teacher, are very strict. Mrs. Deal won't let us chew gum in her class. "The only proper place to chew gum," she says, "is under the bed!" I've never tried that, so I've never found out how proper it is. But then, I can't comprehend a lot of the stuff she talks about. It's like a foreign language to me,

We have to walk downtown to the city hall for our Music, Home Economics, and Shop classes. It doesn't matter if there's rain, sub-zero temperatures, or we're in the midst of a blizzard. We bundle up, drop our heads, and hurry along.

Mr. Newman, our History teacher, was in WW II. He resumed his teaching position when he returned. All we learn in his class is about the war. The boys are very naughty in History class. They throw paper wads in the air and shuffle the desks around the floor with their feet. Round and round the room they go, chanting, "Choo-Choo-Choo!"

Someone in an older class often sticks a funny note on Mr. Newman's back, which makes us laugh. When Mr. Newmen gets mad he pulls all the window shades down. Often the shades are loaded with tiny bits of paper, which float down on him and makes him madder. When he's mad, he reminds me of a rooster flopping around with his head chopped off.

"I went to Mr. Newman's house last night," one student said. "He was throwing report cards up the stairs to determine what grade to put on them." I think about that a lot. I wonder if it is true. I know that many turn in papers from other classes and still get good grades, so maybe it is true.

It is during these days in high school that I am desperately trying to earn my way to Heaven. I do things that I think will please God. I wear my prayer covering and carry my Bible. I don't sing certain songs, dance or go to movies and school parties. I'm very bashful, and only grunt a "good morning" to my classmates. I don't talk much—that is, until I get home.

My classmates are a grand bunch. They are very kind and patient. They accept each one of us as we are. I find more resistance to my odd ways at home than I do at school.

Epilogue—May 28, 2005:

I traveled back to my childhood stomping grounds for the Fiftieth Anniversary of our new High School. Earl Pope met me at the Amtrak in Cumberland, Maryland. When he was elected President of our Senior class fifty years ago he didn't realize it was for the "LONG HAUL." He's done a grand job holding us together. I love being with my classmates! They're an even GRANDER BUNCH today then they were fifty years ago!

I Needed a Friend

"I want a friend of my own," I say as I wipe the sleeve of my dress across my eyes to soak up the tears. "I need a friend!"

"Annie," Mom says, "you and Lydie must share your friends." However, it never works out that way. In the village in which we live most of the kids my age are boys. There are several girls that are between my sister and me, but they prefer my sister. Everyone loves Lydie and no one likes me. She's pretty, I'm not. She knows how to behave and what's proper to do, I don't. She's quiet, I jabber on and on. Then, too, I constantly want my own way. I'm bossy. Everyone says so.

I'm always the one sitting on the top step of the stairway waiting for Lydie and our friend to come out of the locked bathroom. I hear them giggling and speaking in low voices. I want a friend to giggle with and share secrets with. I want a friend of my own. So I cry as I sit on the top step by the bathroom door. If only I had a friend who would prefer being locked in the bathroom with me!

When I bring home a classmate from school to spend the night, it isn't long until I'm trailing in the shadow behind Lydie and my classmate.

"Lydie is very mature," I hear the adults in the village fuss about my sister. "She's a proper young lady and very grown up."

"You can always depend on Lydie."

When Mom leaves for several hours, she always puts Lydie in charge if Sarah is not home. (Sarah's in and out of the hospital a lot.)

"I'm the oldest," I whine. "I ought to be in charge."

When Lydie and I play together she is the leader. I like being with her. I like following her suggestions. I like being her friend. I want to be like her, but I don't like it when my friends prefer her above me.

Wherever we go I look for a set of sisters—an older one with a light complexion with a pretty dark-haired sister. Then I feel sorry for the sister with the light ugly complexion. Surely she is also living in the shadow of a younger sister who knows exactly what, when and where to do the proper things.

Epilogue:

After my own two little girls were grown I became aware that the older was also light-complexioned like me, and the younger one dark. The amazing fact is that the older daughter lived in the shadow of her more self-confident younger sister. But unlike me, my older daughter reached out and nurtured her younger siblings in her growing up years.

A Trip to the Village Store

"Annie," Mom calls from the living room, "Come here!" Mickey Mouse, my cat, and I are nestled comfortably in my favorite spot—Mom's old wicker rocker on the back porch. I stroke the cat a few more times, then rise and drop her to the floor as Mom calls the second time.

"Why can't you come the first time I call?" Mom asks as I step up beside the sewing machine and survey the two heaps beside her chair. I can't tell which is the biggest, the pile already mended or the pile that still needs fixing.

"I want you to run to the store and get me some more black thread," Mom says as she hands me a note. "Now hurry, I don't have much left, and I still have lots of mending to do. Just tell the clerk to write it down on our account."

I take the note and bounce happily down the porch steps and skip down the street. I like running errands for Mom, especially if they take me to the store with its rows and rows of shelves. Two walls have shelves all the way to the ceiling. I like to watch the clerk push the tall stepladder on wheels to the proper place and then mount it to retrieve the merchandise. She has a long thin stick with a hook on the end to help her. I'd like to climb the ladder, too, but customers are not permitted behind the glass counters that contain cookies, candy and all the pretty stuff that's not to be touched.

"Tell your Mom," Dutch, the bossman says as he comes out of the office, "that I'm ready for another one of her pumpkin pies made from carrots." He's our neighbor man across the street.

"I'll take a pumpkin pie too," one of the old men who hangs around the store says. The old men sit around the potbellied stove in the winter, and in the summer they sit on kegs and crates on the long porch. I don't like to walk past them 'cause they always tease me.

"Here you are," the clerk says to me as she hands me a little brown paper bag.

"Write it down," I say, then turn to leave the store. I glance up at the top mailbox cubical on the left as I pass the post office corner in the front of the store. It's empty. One of the other kids must have fetched the mail home already.

I skip down the deserted road toward home. As I get nearer I see Tippy and Mickey Mouse waiting for me. I hurry a bit faster. I love the generous, unconditional welcome they give. It doesn't matter that I've only been gone a few minutes.

A Safety Film

"Have you heard?" Verna asks as she quietly steps in the back door. My sisters and I are helping Mom clean up the kitchen. We've just eaten our noon meal. "The Miller Brother's Machine Shop is holding a community meeting. Everyone is invited." The back door bangs and Frances bustles in out of breath.

"Oh," she laughs. I like to hear her merry chuckles. "You beat me, Verna! Isn't it exciting? It's going to be a potluck dinner."

"What's a potluck dinner?" I ask as I turn from the sink where I'm washing dishes. The wet soggy rag I'm holding drips onto the floor. I flop it back into the dishpan. A surge of water splashes out.

"Annie," Mom scolds. "Watch what you're doing! People will think I haven't taught you anything!"

"Barbara, don't be so hard on her. She's just excited," Verna says. I like Verna. She always sticks up for me.

"No," Mom says." She's just not paying attention to what she's doing." My face turns red as I step into the cellar-way to retrieve the mop from its nail. I gaze at the splash of water on the floor and then quickly mop it up.

"What ya going to take, Barbara?" Verna asks.

"I haven't thought about it yet," Mom says.

"I'm taking my big old moist chocolate cake," Francis says.

"Goodie!" I exclaim. I turn from the sink, but this time I make sure my rag stays inside.

"They are going to show us a film after it gets dark!" Verna says.

"Yes," Francis adds. "It will teach us how to keep our village safe."

I can hardly wait. The whole village is buzzing with excitement. Everywhere I go people are talking about it. There has never been any thing like this before.

The Miller Machine Shop is located on the road that runs up the steep hill past the school. That's the road that goes to Grantsville, Maryland.

When we arrive at the shop the yard is overflowing with people, but there is always room for one more family.

"I've never seen so much food in all my life," I declare to a little fellow with big round eyes. He's following me down the long row of tables. "I can hardly wait 'til it's time to eat!" I say.

"Me too," he lisps.

After we eat, we play games outside while the adults clean up the mess and visit. When it becomes dark, we turn our chairs toward a large screen placed high on the opposite wall of the shop. The lights are turned off and everything becomes quiet. Then music fills the room. I'm awestruck.

Soon different scenes of unsafe practices appear on the screen. Every time a person is about to do something that is not safe, a little big-headed white cartoon character appears on the person's shoulder or stands on an object nearby.

"What are you doing?" the little fellow asks. Then the person recognizes the unsafe thing he is about to do and corrects it.

The next day Mom is recharging the water softener unit in the furthermost corner of our basement. While she works she ponders the strangeness of the little character in the film. She wonders what it would be like to have him appear every time she did something that was unsafe.

I come down the basement steps and walk past Mom, who's pouring rock salt into the softener tank. Her back is turned and she continues to hold the empty bag as she checks the position of the taps. She doesn't seem to know that I'm present, so I tap her on the shoulder and innocently ask, "What are you doing?"

Mom screams, throws her arms above her head, twirls around against the wall and slides to the floor in a swoon.

"Oh," Mom says after she has recovered. "I could have died from a heart attack, and you would never have known that you scared me to death!"

Cousins Galore

"Annie, it's your turn to take a bath," Lydie says as she quietly slips out of the bathroom and heads down the hall. It's Saturday night and time for "Hit Parade." That's when the ten top songs of the week are played on the radio. We listen to it on the little radio iemy brother Moses built before he went into the Marines. It stands on the dresser in the boys' room across the hall from the bathroom. I don't like most of the popular hits, but I do like "On Top Of Old Smoky" and "I'm My Own Grandpa." So I hold still in the tub and listen carefully while these two songs play.

"Oh, goodie!" I splash and make lots of noise. This week both my favorite songs hold a position at the top of the list. As the last song fades away I lie in the warm sudsy tub and ponder the strange possibility of how it might feel to be related to myself. But the fact is, my brothers, my sisters and I are our own cousins many times over, only we don't know it yet—not until years later when my brother Bill (who used to be called Moses) digs into our heritage.

Epilogue:

Someone has described the Amish community as "The Beautiful Web of Intermarriage."

"Huh?" said my brother Bill. "If they think it's beautiful, they should talk to my sister Sally and some of my Mast cousins." One day Bill presented me with twenty-five documented ways in which I am my own cousin within the last five generations. I had, unknowingly, married into my Grandma Diener's family (she and my husband's grandpa are first cousins). So, my own children are more tangled and related to themselves than me. Their ancestry lines cross more then a hundred times. For months our house was filled with the children's playful chant—"I don't have a mommy! I don't have a daddy! I don't have a brother! I don't have a sister! All I have is a bunch of cousins!"

SISTERS: ANNIE & LYDIE DIENER

Camera Shy

Daddy had always been an erect, short, stocky-but-not-fat Amish man with heavy black hair. I miss Daddy's well-trimmed beard now that we're not Amish any more. I wish I had a picture of Daddy as an Amish man, but I didn't have a camera then. I thought he was very handsome, especially when he smiled. I liked to see his gold-capped teeth, which he's had since he was a teenager. That was a long time ago.

I liked Sunday mornings. It was always the same. That's when Daddy came down the stairs dressed in his black church suit with a sparkly white shirt, black suspenders and freshly polished black shoes. Mom made all our clothes when we were Amish, even Daddy's.

Like most Amish men, Daddy didn't like his picture taken. When anyone tried, he'd turn and duck his head. On the other hand, he, as a successful Supplement Feed Salesman, used to strut in front of a camera. Those pictures the company used to advertise their supplements.

Now that we live in Springs we're not Amish anymore, but Daddy still objects to having his picture taken. I saved my allowance and bought a camera, but Daddy won't cooperate.

While Mom is taking a Sunday afternoon nap Daddy loves to put on one of her aprons and pop a big dishpan full of popcorn. He scurries around the kitchen, talking to himself and making funny whistling sounds as he looks for the things he needs. I enjoy the humor he creates. It's not very often I see a man in the kitchen.

One Sunday afternoon I try to take a picture of Daddy in Mom's apron. When Daddy sees me with the camera, he ducks his head and turns his back.

"Come! Come!" I run excitedly to the back porch and call my brother and sisters. "Come! Hold up Daddy's head. I want to take a picture of Daddy in the kitchen." He is stuck and can't leave because the corn is popping furiously. All my camera captures that day is a struggle of many arms, legs and heads, with an apron thrown over the head of the central figure.

Deceptive Dreams

"Annie! GET UP!" Mom's piercing voice resounds up the stairs. "This is the last time I'm calling!" I sit up, startled. The room is full of activity. My sisters are bustling about, preparing for school. I have also been busy—brushing my teeth, combing my hair and slipping into my dress. But then I awake and find that I'm still in bed! It's been another dreadful dream that plagues me. The dream I hate the most is when I think I'm on the toilet and wake up in a wet bed.

A shiver runs through my body. Quickly, I wash my face, brush my teeth and slip into my school dress. When I hear the others leaving the house, tears stream down my face. I wipe them away and flop down in front of the mirror.

"If only this once my straight unruly hair will cooperate," I say to the *strublich,* or unkempt, face in the mirror. Of course, this morning, as usual, my hair has a mind of its own.

"Hurry up!" Mom calls up the stairs, "Or you'll miss the school bus! Oh! Oh!" Mom exclaims. "Here it comes now!" I tumble down the stairs and grab the paper poke Mom holds out. The front door bangs behind me as I rush down the tall porch steps.

I glance across the fields to see the bus fast approaching the village. I run until my sides ache. The bus passes me. I see it pull into the schoolyard to drop off the grade school students it has gathered from across the mountain. Then the village junior and high school scholars mount the bus to be taken to Salisbury Elk Click Joint High School, which is nestled on a high ridge above the little town of Salisbury.

By the time I reach the edge of the schoolyard, the bus is pulling out. The driver stops, opens the door and lets me climb on. I'm huffing and puffing. I'm embarrassed. Everyone is looking at me. I determine not to be late again, but how can I control my dreams?

We Outwit Mom

"Let's make a BIG BIRTHDAY PARTY for Mom," Sarah says one day early in June while Mom's away visiting a neighbor. "She always makes our birthdays special."

"Yippee!" I yell and jump to my feet. "June twenty-fifth is Mom's birthday! Let's surprise her!" I'm excited and full of questions.

"Do you really think we can outwit Mom?"

"How are we going to prepare the food?"

"How are we going to clean and decorate without Mom finding out?"

"How are we going to pass out the invitations?"

And sure enough, as the time draws closer Mom senses something amiss.

"Annie," Mom says one evening, "What's happened to you? Why are you suddenly conscious of the messes you're making? Why are you volunteering to do things that have needed to be done for a long time?"

"I can't figure my children out," I hear Mom say to a neighbor one day. "I've never seen them so conscious of dirt. All of a sudden they enjoy washing windows and scrubbing walls."

"Well, maybe your constant training is finally kicking in," the neighbor lady says with a chuckle. I giggle and run to tell the others. That evening we have a huddled meeting in our bedroom to change our approach.

"Mom! Mom!" Lydie yells from the basement the next day. She and I are using the weekly wash water to scrub down the basement floor and stairs. Mom comes partway down the steps and stands on the platform.

"Look!" Lydie exclaims as she points to the hot water heater across the walkway from the stairs. "Look, what Annie did! She's splashed dirty stair water on the hot water heater!"

"Annie!" Mom exclaims sternly as she props her arms on her hips. "You get a bucket of fresh water and scrub the water heater!" She turns to leave, and then pauses. "While you're at it," she says, "scrub down the deep freeze, water softener and sink also!" When we hear Mom close the basement door Lydie and I bend over and giggle.

Sarah mixes the batter for the birthday cake while Mom and Frances are out hiking. She takes the cake to Verna's house to bake. The punch is mixed and cooling in another neighbor's refrigerator. A few neighbor ladies invite Mom to join them for a leisurely stroll on the day of the party. We scurry to decorate the house and set up tables in the basement for the food. It's cool down there. Then we place extra chairs in the living room.

"Surprise!" everyone yells when Mom walks into the house.

"How did you children manage all this under my nose?" Mom asks. We giggle. "That was more fun and challenging than the party itself," Sarah says. As I listen to the happy buzz and chatter of the ladies and watch Mom enjoy the refreshments and then open her gifts, I think there never has been a better party.

"Where are you going with that chair?" Mom asks as I head out the door with the chair I've been sitting on.

"I'm going to take pictures of your gifts," I say. "There's not enough light in the house." Everyone helps me arrange the gifts on and around the chair, then we position Mom behind it and the happy occasion is forever immortalized in a photo. We are exuberant! We have done it! We have surprised Mom!

A First for Everything

On one of Bill's furloughs home he arrives in a bright red convertible. He's the talk of the neighborhood. One bright sunny day as I walk out of the high school building I see Bill in his convertible parked beside the school buses with the top down. He motions for me to crawl in. I'm afraid to ride with him, but when he motions the second time I timidly slide into the front seat beside him. It is the first time he has ever been nice to me. As we slowly drive away, I hear the kids on the buses and sidewalk "oohing" and "awing."

"Pull my finger," Bill says to me the next day. He's never asked me to do something for him before, so I pull his finger and he *futzhes* (passes gas) and then roars with laughter.

Bill reaches into his pocket and brings out a handful of change. Several coins slip through his fingers. Instinctively, we scramble to retrieve them. Bill bends over and *futzhes* in our faces.

"Ha! Ha! Ha!" Bill roars with laughter. "Keep it," he says.

Bill is busy enlarging Mom's kitchen. I'm amazed as I watch him remove one wall and add another. When he is finished, Mom's new beautiful enlarged kitchen has swallowed up the back porch. He's even halfway decent to us kids. From then on, Bill always brings a new appliance for Mom when he comes home. I am not afraid of him anymore, but I'm not comfortable being around him, either.

Epilogue:

As an adult Bill has been kind to me, although he still wants me to pull his finger. I still cannot speak to him without stuttering, so I remain "Dumb Annie." His pranks have multiplied and spread out among his seventeen nieces and nephews. I now realize it is because I am his sister and he has accepted me that he invites me to pull his finger. He doesn't have this type of relationship with anyone else except his family.

The Early Spring Special

It's happened again! Everyone is talking about it! Many of the outhouses in the community have been tipped over.

"I don't understand," I say, with a whine in my voice. "Why do boys tip over people's toilets?"

"It's because it's Halloween," Mom says, sadly. "On Halloween the big boys do mean tricks to people who do not give them a treat."

"But why?" I ask.

"It's just the way it is," Mom says. "That is why I don't let you dress up on Halloween night and go out 'Trick or Treating.' It just isn't right to force people to give you something, and it isn't right to do mean things to people."

"But can't we dress up funny and go out just one time?" I beg.

"We won't do mean tricks," Lester assures Mom.

"We won't go far away," Lydie says.

"We want to make people laugh," says my littlest sister, Erla.

"Please, Mom. Please let us go." I begin to whine.

"No," Mom says. "Annie, be quiet!" A dead hush fills the room.

"But, I'll tell you what you can do," Mom says. All eyes turn expectantly toward her. "You can go to the store and buy colored construction paper. Tonight we'll sit around the table and weave little baskets. At Easter time you can fill them with colored eggs and candy and then take them to the little children who aren't in school yet. They don't receive Easter treats like you school children do."

"Oh! Goodie! Goodie!" A happy chorus of voices rings out as we clap our hands and dance about. Thus, on every Halloween night we contentedly begin weaving colorful construction paper baskets for our "Early Spring Special!"

Power Struggles

During the winter of the severe snowstorm deep drifts pile up everywhere. Everything stops. Children do not go to school, delivery trucks do not arrive and men do not go to work. A deep hush prevails everywhere. It's as though the world has stopped.

"Yippee," I yell and run through the house. "No school!" I stop at the window between the beds in the girls' room upstairs. Swirls of blowing snow are piling higher and higher.

"Yippee," I yell and whoop some more.

"The hot cocoa is ready," Mom calls from the kitchen. I turn from the window and bounce down the stairs to retrieve my share of the warm soothing cocoa. No one can make it rich and soothing like my Mom.

The storm continues for several days and then the sun shines once more. A quiet lull wraps itself around me. Nothing compares to the beauty and peace of the sparkling, freshly-painted landscape of the high Allegheny Mountains with the crystal blue skies and bright sunshine shining down upon it. I stand by the double dining room windows, nibbling on a piece of toast and absorbing the beauty and tranquillity. Little footprints of birds that have hopped here and there are everywhere.

"They surely weren't looking for worms," I say to my cat, who's sitting on the windowsill in front of me. I've smuggled her into the house. I shove open the window a bit and toss crumbled up toast onto the snow. Instantly the birds return.

"Come, see the birds," I call to the others. A rush of running feet comes from throughout the house. The tiny chirping birds hop here and they hop there. They look up and chirp.

"They're saying 'Thank you,'" I say to my cat as I pick her up and cuddle her in my arms and then drop her to the floor.

"I'm going to build an Eskimo igloo," Lester announces after several beautiful sun-baked days. The loose fluffy snow has settled into heavily packed layers. "I'm going to build it in the empty lot next door."

"Oh! Goodie!" I exclaim as I slap shut the book I'm reading. "I'll help!" That afternoon we cut what seem like hundreds of blocks of snow. Slowly the foundation of a large igloo emerges, but there is also a severe problem—Lester is acting as if he were the boss, but I am the oldest. I ought to be the boss. Of course, Lydie ignores our fuss. She just keeps on doing as she pleases while Lester and I take our contention with us into the house.

"Stop your fighting!" Mom says firmly. "What do you think people will think if you are always fussing at each other? And how do you expect to get to Heaven when you act like this?"

"But I'm the oldest," I whine. "I ought to be the boss!"

"It was my idea," Lester says. "I started it!"

"Stop it," Mom says, "or I'll take one of you and beat the other one up!" That makes Lester and me chuckle and gives Mom a short reprieve.

One by one, the neighborhood guys join us in the building of the igloo. Gradually the girls get pushed out. It takes stronger muscles than we have to lift the heavy snow blocks up onto the rising walls. The problem of who is boss resolves itself. Lester wins and I lose. Lester, of course, has been the boss all along!

When the storm is over, farm tractors and snow plows stack the snow high along the highways. The electric poles and telephone lines are hardly holding their heads above the stacked snow. We neighborhood children make hard-packed slides down the short, steep banks.

The large igloo stands firm until spring. It is a cozy place with a lantern burning in its center. The boys meet in it regularly. We girls and a few younger neighborhood children have our turn in the igloo too. Many happy club meetings are held until the wonderful igloo succumbs to the warm spring breezes that begin to blow across our valley.

Epilogue:

A drunk driver killed my husband in 1981. We still had five dependent children at home. My brother Lester came to my aid and has become my financial advisor and stability. Today, I'm more than happy to pronounce Lester "The BOSS!"

The Finance Games

"Today," I say, shaking a finger into my brother Lester's face, "I'm going to beat you!" He grins and continues counting the money. During the long winter days my brother, sisters and I spend many happy hours around the Finance board. We set the game up on the library table in the living room or on the dining room table. On occasion, a neighborhood kid also joins us.

"Here," Mom says as she comes in from the kitchen with a large dishpan full of fluffy white popcorn. "Don't get too loud," she says, "I'm going to take a nap." I watch her disappear up the open staircase, and then turn back to the business at hand, which, of course, is diving into the gorgeous big pan full of fluffy corn.

"Annie!" Mom calls down the stairs. "Stop being so loud. I can hear you above everybody else. What will people think?" I heave a sigh and try to restrain myself, but it just doesn't work. Lester and I get into a squabble.

"Annie," Mom's stern voice drifts down the stairs again. "How do you expect to get to Heaven when you're continually fighting with your brother? Now stop it!" I run my sleeve across my eyes and let Lester have his way. As usual, I discover that Lester's way is always best.

Our game lasts all afternoon and long into the night. We don't follow the rules according to the game, but obey rules Lester has adopted. He's developed a neat banking system. Of course, Lester always ends up being the king of the Finance board. He graciously bails us less successful businessmen and women out of bankruptcy over and over again.

But in spite of my brother's successful business practices and the lack of mine, I clamber to play every time someone sets up the game. Our common challenge is to bring our brother Lester to his knees. That, of course, never happens. He continues to bail us out of trouble, and not the other way around.

Epilogue:

In real life my brother Lester has become a successful businessman, and he is still reaching out a helping hand to the less fortunate. He claims he has simply applied the basic rules he learned during the long enjoyable winter hours around the Finance board. And me? I'm still sitting at the Finance board, not playing with my brother and sisters, but with my grandchildren. Some I beat and some I don't.

Snow and Hot Cocoa

Throughout the night the snow falls in large quiet flakes. By morning we are snowed in again.

"Yippee!" I yell as I look out the window. "No school today!" By midmorning, a strong wind arises and fills in the low hollows. The temperature drops.

"Yea! Yea!" I yell! I skip! I jump! "We're snowed in!"

"You don't have to worry about frozen pipes and cold furnaces or how to obtain fresh eggs, milk and bread for the table," Mom says. Of course, it seems to me as if Mom is always ready for any emergency. She has a winter's supply of coal tucked into the basement long before the cold weather arrives.

"A deep snow early in the season is good," Mom says. "It insulates the ground."

When the sun shines again, the neighborhood kids meet on our favorite sledding hill. That's the slope on the road that drops out of the village at the Round House gas station. Old-Timers call it the Shoemaker Hill. My sisters and I bundle up in layers of sweaters and our brother's jeans and then stuff ourselves into our long heavy coats.

As I swish down the mile-long slope, I meet groups of kids trudging through the snow, dragging empty sleds behind them. Soon I'm plodding up the long slope also. I never tire of the wonderful free feeling of the fast smooth glide down, down, down and around with the nippy air breezing over my already cold, red face. The swift ride down only takes a fraction of the time or energy required to trudge back to the top, but I do it again and again.

"I'm sweating," I say to Lydie long before we reach the last steep slope. I unbutton my coat and open it briefly to release the pent-up body heat.

Gradually, the slope becomes empty as exhausted, wet, hungry sliders return to the village. My brother, sisters and I crowd in through the back door of our kitchen.

"Go around to the basement with your wet, snow-caked clothes," Mom says as she turns from a large steaming pot of hot coca. "How many times do I have to tell you? Every time you come in?"

The aroma of the smooth, rich cocoa engulfs me. I lick my lips. It's made from our cow's fresh, rich milk. I hurry to crawl out of my snow-caked garments, and then rush up the stairs where large cups of hot steaming cocoa are waiting. I curl my cold fingers around my cup's warmth and take a sip.

"Thank you, Mom," I say, smack my lips, and get lost in the wonderful warmth of my cup's rich, sweet goodness.

Fun in the Mountains

The beautiful sunny snow-covered day glistens and sparkles brightly as I stand by the window, enjoying it's beauty. It's great being in the middle of our winter break from school. Deep, neatly-shoveled paths run though the yard.

"Mom, may I bake an apple pie?" I ask as I turn from the window.

"I don't have time to help you," Mom replies from the rocker in the living room . "I need to finish the mending."

"I know how to bake a pie, Mom! Please?"

"All right," Mom replies, "but make sure you don't get it too sweet."

I grab the dishpan and skip down the basement stairs. The apple bin is in the far corner. I fill the pan quickly, then scramble back up to the kitchen, plop it on the table and slip into Mom's apron. As I begin to peel the apples, a song springs into my heart and I sing like Mom does when she works in the kitchen! I mix the flour, salt and lard together and then moisten it with water.

"Making spicy apple pie is easy!" I say to Tippy, our dog, who's come to the kitchen to investigate the racket I'm making. Mom allows him in the house when it's cold.

"This is fun!" I say to Tippy as I grin and slide my pie into the oven. I set the timer and then run off to play.

"Ping!" I rush into the kitchen and peek inside the oven door. My pie is a golden brown. I flop down a hot pad on the counter and set my pie out to cool. Several hours later, we gather in the kitchen to enjoy my first pie. I skip down the basement steps the second time to fetch the large pail of ice cream from the tall upright freezer. However, the pie crust is so tough no one can cut through it.

"Here, try this," my brother Bill says as he hands me the hatchet from the barn. He's home on leave from the Air Force. I burst into tears.

The pie sits on the cupboard untouched for several days. Sarah's friend, Susan, comes to visit. Susan is tall and extremely heavy.

"Hum," Susan says when she sees the untouched pie. "Apple pie! I love apple pie!" She grabs a knife, cuts a large piece and devours it. I guess the crust has absorbed some moisture. By the end of her visit, the pie is eaten, crust and all.

"That girl is at least two ax handles wide," Bill says after she's gone.

"Don't talk that way, Bill!" Mom says. "She's Sarah's friend."

"Well, I can't help she's so big and fat!"

"Bill!" Mom says sharply.

"OK! OK!" Bill holds up his hands to ward off Mom. "The next time she comes I'll bring in the ax and you can measure her yourself."

A few days later Susan is back. We are bundling up to take Mom's car over the mountain ranges. We're going sledding! The back door opens quietly.

"Here, Mom," Bill says as he sets the large long-handled ax beside the door. Mom turns red with embarrassment. We kids double over laughing. Susan has no clue, so she laughs too. In the midst of the gales of laughter, several neighborhood kids and us hook our sleds on the bumper and pile into the car.

"Oh no!" We groan in unison. Susan is coming out of the back door bundled in her heavy black coat.

"I'm coming," she calls. She opens the back door and shoves herself in. We get squished and squeezed on top of each other. When we reach the first tall mount, Lester stops the car. We roll out and unhook our sleds. With a running start I slam down on top of my slide. The ride is fast. The high snowbanks slip swiftly past. The car follows behind, and gradually the sleds come to a stop as they start climbing the next slope. I hook my sled on the bumper again and crawl back into the car. Susan is sound asleep on the back seat. We pile in on top of her. At every summit someone else takes a turn driving the car.

We spend a lovely cool sun-filled afternoon in the mountains while Susan sleeps on and on and on. When we arrive home and roll out of car Susan awakes. Mom has a large pot of hot cocoa waiting for us.

"Wow!" Susan says as she returns to the pot for seconds, then thirds. "We certainly have had a wonderful day sliding in the mountains!"

Free Eggs!

The Old Order Amish families in the area will not sell anything to or eat or buy anything from my folks because they left the Amish Church in Illinois. The Church "miting" has been put on our family. I don't know what that means except that it makes my Mom cry.

"Annie," Mom calls up the stairs. My younger sisters and I are locked in our bedroom, playing with our paper doll families. "We're out of eggs," Mom says. "The egg truck cannot get through. You and Lester bundle up and go to the nearest farm and buy us some eggs." I see Mom giving Lester some money as I come tumbling down the stairs.

The farm we head for is not far from the village. I drop my head low and follow Lester through the knee-high snowdrifts. A strong wind is blowing pelts of icy crystals into my face, making it "ting." I lift my arms in a useless attempt to shield my face. A sudden strong gust of wind hits us and we automatically turn our backs. It's awkward walking backward in deep snow.

I'm glad when we finally reach the farm and climb onto the protection of the back porch. Lester knocks loudly on the door, and the lady invites us in.

"We're out of eggs," Lester says boldly. "Can we buy some eggs from you?"

"I'm sorry," the lady says. "We don't have any eggs."

Just then two boys step into the back door. Each of them is carrying a large wire basket full of eggs. A quiet hush falls over the room.

"I'm sorry," the lady says quietly. She turns a deep scarlet red. "I didn't know we had eggs!" She quickly counts out several dozen and places them in our container.

"Here is your money," Lester says as he holds it out to her.

"No," she says softly as she shakes her head. "You don't need to pay." Lester stuffs the money back into his pocket.

"Don't worry about it," Mom says when we tell her what happened. "It'll go home with her." Mom hurries to her room and I hear her crying. I don't know exactly what Mom means, but I do know, as I listen to her sobs, that it has something to do with the "shunning" and "church miting." That's why we left our family in Illinois and moved to Pennsylvania. Will we need to move again? I ponder the problem for a long time with fear gripping my heart.

Too Many Soap Suds

The tragedy occurred the first time I was responsible to prepare a small lunch for Lynn. I've never forgotten it and I often wonder if he has.

Around the first large curve as you come toward Springs is a large brick quarry. It is owned and operated by the Otto brothers. Many of the men in the little village are employed at the Otto Brick Works. Two of the Otto brothers, Roy and Walter, are the ministers in our little community church. They take turns preaching.

Roy and Melda have a young five-year-old son, Lynn, as well as two grown children. I occasionally have the privilege of babysitting for Lynn.

"I'm going to wash the dishes," I say as I get up from the table after we're finished eating our small meal. I put the plug into the kitchen sink, squeeze in a squirt of soap and turn on the water to wash the two bowls, two cups, three spoons and the small pan I used to heat the soup.

"Mama washes the dirty dishes in here," Lynn says as he points to a strange-looking appliance standing beside the sink.

"You have a machine that washes dirty dishes?" I ask in amazement as I fiddle with the levers and buttons in an attempt to open its door. "I didn't know there was such a thing!"

"Here it is!" Lynn says as he hops off his chair, pulls a lever and watches as the lid pops open. I place our two bowls, two glasses, two spoons, the pot and small dipper inside.

"Put the soap in there," Lynn points to a tiny container on the dishwasher wall. I reach under the sink, retrieve the regular dish soap and squirt the soap container full. To make sure the dishes get clean, I squirt some over the dishes, also, and then close the lid. Lynn shows me which dial to turn. I hear water coming into the dishwasher. Soon I hear it swish and swirl around.

Gradually the sound of the swishing water fades away, and little bubbles of soap suds begin creeping through the door seal. They come and come and come. I grab a dishpan and slap it full of suds and then run out the back door and dump the pan of suds on the grass. When I come back into the kitchen heaps of suds are on the floor. "Quick," I call to Lynn, "get something and help carry out the suds!" We run back and forth, back and forth as the dishwasher continues to spit out its suds. Lynn thinks its fun, but I'm horrified. I'm afraid I've ruined his mama's brand new dishwashing machine.

When Melda returns there's a mountain of soapsuds by her back door. She has a hearty laugh.

"I'm afraid I've ruined your new dishwasher," I say.

"Come," she says as she leads me to the dishwasher and shows me where, how much and what kind of soap to put in, but I never attempt to wash the dishes the easy way again.

Epilogue:

Years later I returned to Springs to attend my thirty-fifth high school graduation banquet. My sister Erla, who had come with me, and I stopped to see our beloved pastor and his wife. She teased me about my dish-washing abilities and assured me that I had not ruined her machine. It was still sitting in her kitchen, still producing the proper amount of suds and keeping her dishes sparkling clean.

Generous Bags of Potato Chips

Sarah and her friend Betty Durst have gone through school together. Betty's family lives beyond our farm as you go up the mountain toward Mount Davis. Betty's mom is a wonderful seamstress. She buys washed and pressed feed sacks from my mom and fashions beautiful, tailored dresses for Betty.

"The dresses your mama makes," I say to Betty every time she appears with a new one, "are prettier then the ones in the Sears Roebuck Catalog." In fact, I'd rather have one of Betty's dresses than any I see in the catalog. Mom makes my dresses out of bags too, but they're not fancy like Betty's. So I copy Betty's dresses as I tailor clothes for my own little doll, Betty Elizabeth.

After Betty graduates from high school, she works in the little Community Store in the center of Springs. "Dutch," our neighbor, owns the store. She earns lots of money—seventeen dollars a week. During her lunch break she comes to our house.

Every day at noon (when there is no school) I sit on the tall front porch steps and watch for Betty to come down the street. What I'm really watching for is the big bag of potato chips she always brings.

"Here she comes!" I yell.

"Does she have potato chips?" someone asks.

"Yes," I reply. The others join me and we hop, whoop and holler as we rush off the porch to meet Betty. Tippy is the only decent one among us. He stays at the edge of the yard and doesn't make any noise.

"The way you carry on," Mom calls after us, "people will think all you want are her potato chips." But we pay no attention to Mom as we cluster around Betty, chattering like monkeys.

"I'll carry the bag of chips!" I offer as I reach for them. In the kitchen we find Mom dipping bowls of soup.

"Here, Betty," Mom hands her the first bowl. Then Betty opens the large bag of chips and our Saturday feast begins. I think Betty is very rich. We don't get potato chips very often, that is, unless Betty comes. So Betty and her generous bags of potato chips earn a special spot in my heart forever.

UFOs?

"Don't stand around and talk forever," Mom says as she herds us out the front door. "Remember, there's school tomorrow." My brother, my sisters and I skip down the front steps and chatter merrily as we head for the elementary school. We're on our way to our monthly MYF meeting. That stands for Mennonite Youth Fellowship.

There aren't very many of us, but we have lots of fun. We often divide into two teams and have exciting relays and quizzes. It's challenging to try to be the last one standing, especially if Claude and Freda join in. They're part of the sponsorship. It's hard to beat them.

We stay until Verd Yoder, the school custodian, comes to lock up. She lives across the little dirt road from the school. The road has a deep ditch running along the side of her yard. I like to skip across her little footbridge to visit her. She's lots of fun. Verd knows everything about nature. She doesn't think I ask too many questions and neither is she in a hurry to "shoo" me home.

After our MYF meeting is over and the school is locked, we stand in a cluster around Verd. We gaze into the night sky and follow the stars in their courses as she expounds them to us.

"Verd," one of the boys ask, "do you think there are flying saucers or UFOs up there in the sky like they say on the radio?"

"I can't say yes or no," Verd says. "The wonders of God's creation are full of surprises! I really don't know."

"My Mom says they're just made-up stories to scare people," one of the boys say.

"Oh, I don't know," Verd replies. "But, I do know that God is great and all-powerful. He may have another universe out there somewhere! There may be people out there much smarter than us." We stand gazing into the darkened cloudy sky. Only a few stars appear here and there. There is complete silence. Everyone is wrapped in their own thoughts. Suddenly, a cloud is illuminated in a beam of light and held in its grip above our heads. Light refracts in every direction.

"Aah," a soft gasp of astonishment floats across our group. I stand transfixed as fear grips my chest and tightens it. Stillness surrounds me. Then, as quickly as it came, the light vanishes as a car comes to the crest of the hill and its beams fall on us.

"Oh!" Verd laughs. "There for a minute I thought we were witnessing an UFO. But it was only the headlights of a car shining into the night sky as it came over the crest of the hill." We laugh, then turn and head home.

New Butter on the Market

A BIG question mark plops itself right into my head. Our chemistry teacher has just said that someday we are going to be eating artificial food.

"How can that be?" I ask one of my classmates as we file out of his room and prepare to catch our buses to go home. "How can food be artificial?" My mind flies to the large bowl of colorfully painted wooden fruit sitting on our dining room table at home.

"Will someone mix chemicals like we do in our chemistry lab until an apple or something else pops out?" I ponder the mystery all the way home.

"Kids," Mom calls as we enter the front door. "Hurry and change your clothes. The butter churn is waiting on the back porch! Annie, you go first."

I plop down beside the big wooden churn and begin turning the crank. I like to hear the "splash-splash" of the cream as it swishes around inside. Soon my brother comes to relieve me. When it's my turn again, the sound has changed. Little chunks of butterfat are sticking together and becoming bigger and bigger as they tumble through the buttermilk. When fat chunks of butter fall with a heavy thud, the churn becomes imbalanced and hard to turn.

"That's enough," Mom says. She lifts the churn to the edge of the sink. "Get a glass." I lick my lips as I rush to the cupboard. Mom opens a small spout at the bottom of the churn and slowly fills the glass with refreshing cool buttermilk. We each get several turns sipping it.

"Oh! You've made butter!" Frances, our neighbor, says as she rushes in the back door. Mom hands her a tall glass of buttermilk.

"Barbara, did you hear the news?" Frances asks, after she's taken a sip.

"No," Mom says. "I haven't had the radio on."

"Well," Frances says with gusto. She loves to be the first to pass bits of news around. "The dairy farmers are upset about this new vegetable spread that has hit the market. It's something like butter. They call it Oleo Margarine. They're afraid it will affect the butter sales, so they've asked the government to not allow yellow dye to be put into it."

"Why?" I ask.

"Because the dye will make it look like butter."

Mom removes the big chunk of bright yellow butter briskly from the churn and places it into a large bowl with a flop. She runs cold water over it and begins kneading it with her fingers, squeezing out the last bits of buttermilk. When the water becomes milky, she replaces it with fresh. Soon she has a beautiful large yellow hunk of butter ready to be salted and then pressed though her pound mold.

"How can there be butter that doesn't come from cream?" I ask.

Mom turns and holds out her buttery fingers for us kids to lick. I've been licking her butter fingers ever since I can remember. Mom grins at Frances and then washes her hands. I see the butter mold standing by the sink. It's a small wooden box with a removable bottom. Mom presses out oblong pounds of butter in it, and then wraps them neatly in thin sheets of butter paper.

"How can there be butter that doesn't come from cream?" I ask again.

"I don't know," Mom says as she hands me the platter of freshly wrapped butter blocks. "Place this in the refrigerator." As I shove the tray into the refrigerator, I know that Mom's butter will sell quickly.

"That new stuff called Oleo Margarine surely won't sell in this village," I say as I slam the door shut, but I'm wrong. Even Mom begins to buy the white oleo stuff for us to eat, so she has more butter to sell. It's much cheaper than butter. I watch her mix the little packets of yellow powder into it. When she's done, it looks like butter, but it tastes different. Mom fixes that by adding more salt. Every time I lick Mom's oleo fingers I wonder if this is the artificial food my chemistry teacher was talking about.

A Discovery!

Algebra I is a required class. Other sophomores and I file into Mr.Newman's room at the top of the stairs on the second floor for a fresh challenge in algebra every day. Mr.Newman is also our homeroom teacher.

"The office needs to see everyone's birth certificate," Mr.Newman announces one afternoon before dismissing us for the day. I've never seen my birth certificate, so I'm in awe when Mom permits me to carry it to school the next day.

"Anna," Mr.Newman says as he looks up from the stack of birth certificates. "According to this, your name is not Anna, but Anne!" That surprises me. So in school from that day on I am Anne.

Algebra frightens me. It sounds like something not belonging to this world. But Mr.Newman has a special way of presenting the subject and making the class challenging. I soon relax and algebra becomes my favorite subject.

"I have a riddle for you," Mr.Newman says frequently before we plunge into the mysterious methods of algebra. I sit up straight. I love the challenge of a good riddle.

"Take it home and sleep on it," Mr.Newman says. "Let's see how many of you can figure it out by tomorrow's class." It's hard to lay the riddle aside and concentrate on the algebra problems. The riddle keeps popping back into my mind all through English and History classes. Typing class doesn't go well, either. In the afternoon we walk in little clusters down the hill to the Town Hall for our weekly music class. The others chatter, but my mind is on the riddle. During music class I find it hard to sing and think about the riddle at the same time.

"What's wrong with you, Annie?" Mom asks as we're eating supper. "Why are you so quiet? Are you sick?" I tell them the riddle, but no one is interested in helping me solve it. I toss all night and am the first one up in the morning.

"Why, Annie!" Mom exclaims. "You're the first one down for breakfast! What makes you so perky this morning?"

"Mr. Newman is going to give us the answer to the riddle. I don't want to miss the bus! I think I have the answer!" I exclaim as I empty my bowl of oatmeal, grab my lunch sack and pick up my stack of books. The front door slams behind me as I rush down the porch steps toward the road. I'm early. I'm anxious to get to school.

In my senior year, a new high school is built by the village park. We move in at the beginning of the second semester. During Christmas break, the senior class uses Earl Pope's daddy's farm tractor and hay wagon to transfer boxes and stacks and stacks of books from the library on the hill onto their new shelves in the village park. Yea! Yea! No more walking down the steep hill in bad weather for our Music, Shop and Home Ec. classes.

Epilogue:

I was born at home. "It's a girl!" the doctor said to Mom. "What's her name?"

"Annie!" Mom replied. The doctor took the statistics and drove back to his office, where his secretary recorded the facts. Somehow the "i" was left out. When I entered school *Annie* was given the English translation of *Anna*—until the discovery was made in high school that my name was, indeed, *Anne*! From plain little "Annie" with no middle name, I suddenly became, "Anna Anne Annie!" (Now that I'm a grandma, my southern grandbabies have added *Nana* to my list of names. I'm sad to report that Anna Anne Annie has not retained any of Mr. Newman's challenging riddles.

Inspirational Tent Meetings

"Please, Mom. We want to watch the big tent go up!" My brother, sisters and I are jumping up and down in front of Mom. "Please? Please take us to see the big tent! Please?"

The Hammer Tent Revival Meetings have come to our community. A huge canvas tent is being erected in a hay field on the road going toward Grantsville, Maryland.

"Please, Mom. We want to watch the big tent go up!" Mom stops what she's doing, wipes her hands on her apron and takes it off.

When we arrive the field is swarming with people—many of whom I've never met—surrounding a big heap of canvas.

"Whoa!" I declare. "That's the biggest hunk of canvas I've ever seen!" My eyes are wide with amazement as it is being stretched out on the ground by dozens of men.

"Come," says Mom, "let's get a little closer." I follow Mom through the crowd. Slowly and carefully, the largest tent I've ever seen is erected. Tall poles with rows of lights on them hold up the tent. A large tall platform with steps is assembled across one end. Deep sawdust is strewn across the meadow floor, and roughly hewn benches are placed in long, tight rows with one wide central isle. Behind the platform is the prayer room. That's where I will be spending a lot of time during the next few weeks. I want to make sure I can go to Heaven when I die.

"Let's go home," Mom says. "We have lots to do before we can come back for the first service." I fly through my chores that evening.

"Whoa! Annie!" Mom says. "This is a switch! I don't need to probe you on and on to get your work done!" I smile. I'm thinking of the big tent and how it'll feel to sit in it.

When we arrive, the field is already full of parked cars. We have to park a long distance away, but I don't mind. People are everywhere. There's excitement in the air as a new chapter in my life begins.

I sit packed among the people night after night, singing with luster and listening to Brother Hammer expound the Word of God though a loudspeaker that stands by the rough-hewn pulpit. My heart is touched. My love and desire to please God is increased, and I determine to follow God more closely.

Over the next several years many large tent meetings are held in our community or in communities within reach. We charter buses to take us to Johnstown and other distant points to hear Brother Hammer or the Brunk Brothers. One summer the community drives to Pittsburgh to hear a young minister by the name of Billy Graham. The arena is full, with not even standing room left. We crowd around the open doors and windows to get a glimpse and hear his voice.

Even in all these good meetings, I do not grasp that it is by God's grace and His grace alone whereby I am saved. So, I add wearing my head covering continually and carrying my Bible wherever I go to my already long list of religious duties.

"When I grow up I'm going be a missionary," I declare boldly. Surely missionaries go to Heaven!

Epilogue:

I'm thankful I was not strong enough in character to follow through with the decisions I made in my youth. I could have spent my life depriving myself and serving others, and then died and gone to hell because I had clung tightly to a bag full of do's and don'ts instead of to HIM. It was not until I was an adult that God, by His Grace, enabled me to dump that rotten bag of wretchedness at Jesus' feet and say—"Here am I. Fill me with your own precious self."

Utter Despair

"Give it to me!" I snatch at the newspaper Lester is reading. "I want to see!" I whine and stomp my foot. Lester turns his back and keeps on reading while I pound my fist into his shoulders.

"Annie! Stop that!" Mom says as she steps into the dining room where Lester has the newspaper spread out on the dining room table in front of him. "You go find something else to do." I go out on the back porch and flop into Mom's rocker. Mickey Mouse, my cat, jumps into my lap and begins to purr.

I've failed again. I'll never make it to Heaven. If Mom is not pleased with me, surely God is not either. Worst of all, no one wants to be around me. I groan. Despair grips me with its icy fingers and tears run down my face as I get up and head for the woods. Mickey Mouse follows me.

"I love you, God," I tell him. "But how am I going to get to Heaven?" I cry out my sorrow to God as I walk among the trees and rocks. God somehow comforts me, but I don't understand how to be accepted by Him. So again, I set higher standards for myself.

"Surely now," I say to Mickey Mouse as we head back toward the house, "I'll be able to go to Heaven when I die." I sing and skip along. But the higher I set my standards, the further, deeper and harder I fall into another pit of hopeless despair and the more unfavorable I become to my family and friends.

Epilogue:

I was an adult—twenty-six years old—before I understood that it is God, not me, who does the cleansing and the saving, and it is He, not me, that keeps me. With my hand in His, the joy and fellowship of His Word bubbles within as I skip down the path of life. I'm never alone. The joy and exuberance of His presence surrounds me and wherever I go; I feel safe, accepted, and loved.

I've Striven to Obtain God's Favor

I listen intently while Mom reads the continued story "Light From Heaven." I can hardly wait each week for the church paper to arrive. I want to be like the little boy in the story. I want to be approved of God like he was. Maybe, if I do everything just right I, too, can go to Heaven. So I set rules for myself, but I soon discover that I cannot keep my own rules.

"Annie, is that the way a Christian should act? What will people think?" Mom's frequent reminders cut deep into my heart like a knife. Would I ever attain my goal of getting to Heaven? I know God certainly can't accept me the way I am! I'm sure of that.

My heart aches. I love God and I want to go to Heaven, so I continue to make rigid rules and regulations for myself. I read my Bible, pray and witness to children. I go to church, wear my head covering and carry my Bible wherever I go. I refuse to watch television, go to school parties or basketball games. I don't do this! I don't do that!

But the higher I build my platform of righteousness, the greater and more frequent is my fall into hopeless despair.

"Oh!" I cry in horror one morning. I've gone three days without praying or reading my Bible, and I didn't even realize it till now! The bedroom is empty and everyone else is already up and gone. I throw myself on the bed and weep. I'll never make it to Heaven! My heart is broken.

"Oh God," I turn my face into my pillow and cry, "I can't keep myself saved! Surely I'll never get to live with you in Heaven! But God, I don't want to go to Hell!"

I realize I'm fast becoming a "Goodie, Goodie, Two Shoes" that no one wants to be around, and Mom's sharp words of reproof cut deep into my heart.

"Annie," she says a half-dozen times a day, "is this the way a Christian should act? How do you expect to get to Heaven if you act that way?" Her words sting as they sink into the depths of my soul and cause me to cringe as another wave of hopelessness engulfs me.

Epilogue:

God's Grace was able to peel off all the layers of "self-righteousness" that I had wrapped myself in and implant HIS RIGHTEOUSNESS into my soul. His cleansing JOY has been bubbling in my life ever since. I haven't been perfect, but I've learned that my strength and joy come from God and HIS WORD—from Him and Him alone—and not from the things that I do or don't do!

A Rotten Bag Full of Holes

During the days when I am desperately trying to obtain favor with God by doing things to please Him I go to church, wear my head covering all the time, read my Bible and pray everyday, and frequently talk to someone about God.

There are things I don't do. I don't roll my stockings down nor my sleeves up like others are doing. I don't listen to the radio nor watch TV at the neighbors. I don't sing worldly songs, dance or go to the movies.

But it is TV that gets me into trouble with my family. We don't have one in our home, so we frequently go over the mountain to our friends' house to enjoy an evening of TV entertainment. I find excuses not to go.

"Come on, Annie," Mom calls from the back door. "Everyone is in the car. We're waiting on you!"

"I can't go tonight," I call down the stairs. "I have a school project that is due tomorrow."

"Well, OK," Mom replies. "We'll be back by bedtime." But this strategy doesn't work very long. Mom soon catches on.

"If everyone doesn't go, no one will go!" Mom says one evening. Now I have my brother and sisters on my back. So I go. I stay in the kitchen doing my school projects or reading a book. I have to walk through the living room to go to the outhouse, pump a drink of water from the well or check on the time. The clock is on the wall above the TV. The evening drags by slowly, and I check the time frequently.

"Annie," one of my siblings says on the way home, "I saw you peeking around the corner trying to watch TV."

"No, I wasn't. I was looking what time it was."

"Oh yes, you were," they all chirp in. I wipe my eyes on my upper sleeve and try to fight back the flood of water that is threatening to burst from them.

"Well, I'm not going to prayer meeting if 'Goodie, Goodie, Two Shoes' goes," one of my siblings says the next evening. Mom often makes me stay home so that they will go. I feel lonely. I cry a lot. I take long walks deep into the woods behind our property and cry out my sorrow and loneliness to God. I feel His presence and somehow he comforts me. I determine not to let loose of my self-imposed standards, for how else can I be assured a home in Heaven?

During the summer of my sophomore year in high school, I apply to the Mennonite Mission Board for "Voluntary Youth Service." I am sent to Youth Village near White Pigeon, Michigan. It is a camp for underprivileged children from Chicago. I stay all summer. I work in the laundry. A college student and I use an old-fashioned ringer washing machine and hang the clothes out on lines. In the afternoon we iron and deposit the clothes back into the proper cabins. We do a different set of cabins every day.

My heart sings for joy as I serve in the laundry, help in the dining room, go to the swimming beach with the girls and help with craft projects. Before bedtime each night we sit around a bonfire. The leaders give Bible lessons and teach meaningful songs and choruses. I weep often for joy, for surely now I will be able to go to Heaven when I die, but some of my fellow workers think I'm homesick.

In the fall when I return home a truce has been made, and I am permitted to do the things I'm convicted in my heart to do.

Epilogue:

It was not until after I was grown and a mother myself that the Holy Spirit was able to bring me to the end of all my self-righteousness. It was then that I cried, "God, be merciful to me, a sinner, and save me, for Jesus' sake!"

That day a shaft of light from Heaven entered my darkened soul with the promise, "I will never leave thee or forsake thee."

In that flash of light I saw that it was God's Righteousness, not mine, that I needed to lean on. My self-righteousness has been a rotten bag full of holes dropping rotten rags all over the place.

And so, with JOY I've been walking and rejoicing in God's righteousness and cleansing Light ever since.

#1 Ball Player

"I've bought a double lot in Florida," Daddy announces one day. He's just come home from another trucking trip.

"What did you do that for?" Mom asks.

"I stopped to see my brother Amos and his family. They like it there. A lot of Amish are moving to Florida. It stays warm during the winter. I figured you might want to move there too."

"I wouldn't like the heat in the summer," Mom says, "I'd rather stay here."

"Can we take Tippy and Mickey Mouse?" I ask.

"No animals," Daddy says. Right there and then I put in my negative vote on the move to Florida. The others weren't crazy about it either.

That summer Tippy learns to play ball. The neighborhood kids play what we call "High-Fly" with us. Any board or club makes a fine bat. A high-fly ball that is caught "out'ens" the whole team, while a first bouncer out'ens the batter. A ball that is thrown in front of a runner out'ens him, unless he turns his back on the ball as he is running. Three "outs" and the team's batting turn is over.

"Junior and I'll be the captains," Lester says. He picks up the bat and throws it to Junior, who catches it with one hand. Then they walk their hands up the bat. The hand that clutches the top chooses first.

I enjoy playing in the neighborhood ball games. However, when Tippy decides to join, our fun increases. He catches high-flies and out'ens the team. He catches first bouncers and out'ens the runner. He grabs up grounders and runs head-smack into the runner. That eliminates him too. Most of the games are played in our pasture, so Tippy can be part of the fun. It is clear that the team who claims Tippy always wins. He's the #1 player.

Pesky Persistent Feelings

In the spring of my senior year, a registered nurse comes to our Home Economics class and teaches us the basic principles of nursing. We learn how to read a thermometer, give bed baths and backrubs, and make a proper bed. I can't shake the feeling that I should become a nurse, but I don't want to be a nurse. I don't want to be around sick people. I don't want to go to school for four more years, so I don't talk about it. I try to forget the pesky persistent feelings I have.

"What's wrong with you, Annie?" Mom asks.

"Nothing," I say and run upstairs and throw myself on my side of the bed and cry and cry and cry. I refuse to eat. Then I become sick.

"I'm going to call the doctor," Mom says.

"No," I wail, "don't call the doctor!" Finally, after several miserable days, I yield to the inner voice encouraging me to become a nurse. I take a bath, comb my hair and join my family at the dinner table.

"I'm going to become a nurse after I graduate," I announce. "I'm going to go to Goshen College, just like Sally!"

"Well," Mom says, "if all you kids are going to Goshen College, I'm going to move there too. We'll be close to Daddy's headquarters." A cheer goes up from around the table. We've met some of our Indiana cousins and have been begging Mom to move.

"We can't take any animals," Mom says. "Our house will be in town." That puts a damper on our joy.

"Well," I say, "if Tippy and Mickey Mouse can't go, I'm not going!" The others don't want to leave Tippy behind, either, so talk about moving ceases.

A Sad Time

Soon afterward, a dreadful dog disease moves through the village. Our Tippy becomes ill. Mom takes him to the vet.

"There's a lot of life left in that dog," the vet says. Mom brings him home and puts his box in the basement.

"Mom! Mom!" I scream the next morning. I've gone to the basement to check on my friend. "Tippy is dead!" I collapse over the box and wail. There's a stampede of feet throughout the house as everyone rushes to the basement.

We bury him under the old apple tree and our home becomes a sad, quiet place. Everyone is grieved, even the cats! They keep meeting us after school at the road, but things are not right without Tippy.

Now we are willing, even anxious, to enter into the adventure of another move. Daddy backs his big blue and white moving van up to the back porch and moves us to 758 East Market Street, Nappanee, Indiana. I enroll in the nursing program at Goshen College that fall. My brother Bill moves home and also enrolls. Bill, my sister Sally and I commute together the first year. After that I am required to live in the dorm.

Epilogue:

It was great being near Daddy's headquarters and seeing him often. However, a severe problem soon arose and Mom and Daddy divorced. The trauma left me emotionally broken, and I was unable to finish my training.

I'm Embarrassed

I am in my second year of Nurse's Training at Goshen College when Mom's Aunt Lizzy dies.

"Telephone call on line three for Anna Diener," the speaker in the ceiling of the second floor hallway announces one evening. I mark my place in the textbook, slide back my chair and skip down the stairs into the main lobby. It's Mom. She wants me to meet her at the hospital across the street from my dorm room. I wait twenty minutes to give her time to arrive, then I cross the busy highway

When I arrive, the waiting room is full of Mom's old uncles and first cousins. I don't know them very well, but of course, they have visited our home over the years. As I walk toward the group two of Mom's old uncles get up and wobble toward me.

"*Vow bish du*?" (Who are you?)

"*Vow bish du*?" they ask as they slowly approach, leaning on their canes.

"*Meir seta dich visa*!" (We should know you.)

"*Vow bish du*?" I'm baffled. I cannot answer.

Then I hear a little tiny thin voice saying, "*Ich ben de Barbie ouw gla maile.*"" (I am Barbara's little girl.) I am embarrassed. Quickly I wipe away a few tears.

"*Yaw, yaw*," (yes, yes) they say, turn and hobble back to their seats. Then Mom comes in the door. I've never been happier to see her. I fade into the background as I always do among hosts of relatives that I don't really know.

Well, Aunt Lizzy dies, and relatives come from far and near for the funeral. For several days our living room on Market Street in Nappanee, Indiana, is packed with visiting relatives. They reminisce about Aunt Lizzy. My ornery brother, Bill, who used to be called Moses in my growing up years, has moved back home. He's also attending Goshen College. His bedroom opens into the living room, and every time a fresh batch of relatives arrives at the house he steps out of his bedroom.

"Mom," he says, rubbing his chin, "who is every one talking about? It seems as if I should know this Lizzy. Ohhh, yes!" he tilts his head up with a triumphant look. "I remember! Wasn't she the one who came to visit us the fall while we lived in Pennsylvania on the farm and were snowed in until Spring? That was Aunt Lizzy, wasn't it? Didn't she refuse to take a bath all winter because she was afraid of getting sick? Yes, yes, I remember now. Yes, I do!" Bill turns and ducks into his room. The living room is deathly quiet. Mom is embarassed. Gradually, the conversation picks up again.

"Bill!" Mom closes the front door and walks toward Bill's room after the last visitor has left. "What did you do that for?"

"Do what?" Bill asks, insulating an innocent look on his face.

"You know what I'm talking about!"

"Well, it's true isn't it?" Bill throws his head back and laughs. The doorbell rings and Mom ushers in another set of visitors. And, with each new set of visitors, Bill does the same thing to poor Mom.

Photos of Annie

Precious Memories

Precious mem'ries, unseen angels,
Sent from somewhere to my soul;
How they linger, ever near me,
And the sacred past unfold.

Precious Father, loving Mother,
Fly across the lonely years;
And old home scenes of my childhood,
In fond memory appears.

In the stillness of the midnight,
Echoes from the past I hear,
Oldtime singing, gladness bringing,
From that lovely land some-where.

I remember Mother praying,
Father too, on bended knee;
Sun is sinking, shadows falling,
But their pray'rs still follow me.

As I travel on life's pathway,
Know not what the years may hold;
As I ponder, hope grows fonder,
Precious mem'ries flood my soul.

Precious mem'ries, how they linger,
How they ever flood my soul,
In the stillness of the midnight,
Precious, sacred scenes unfold.

~

~by J.B.F. Wright

Yes, As Far Back As I Can Remember—

I've Yearned to Belong to God

Yes, I love God, and His Word.
Yes, I spend time conversing with Him daily.
Yes, I attend Church services
and sing praises to Him from my heart.
Yes, I take all my cares and burdens to Him.
and He mercifully lifts them one by one.
Yes, He has graciously guided me down through the years,
and placed my feet on solid places.
Yes, I've come to know the Lord of Love,
and experienced unbroken union with Him.
And now, I don't have to remember back,
for the LORD GOD is always with me
And through His Holy Spirit He reminds me-
THAT I AM HIS
and
HE IS MINE
Now and forever more,
throughout all eternity!

World without end!
Amen!!

Treasure In An Earthly Vessel

As an adult
twenty-six years of age
the
LORD GOD
He has found me
changed me
into the person
He wants me to be
—softly
—quietly
granting stability
with
Peace and Quietness
Forever!
World Without End!
Amen

Psalm 90

LORD, thou hast been our dwelling place in all generations.

Before the mountains were brought forth, or ever thou hadst formed the earth and the world, *even from everlasting to everlasting, thou art GOD*...

For a thousand years in thy sight are but as yesterday when it is past, and are as a watch in the night.

Thou carriest them away as with a flood; they are as a sleep: in the morning they are like grass which groweth up.

In the morning it flourisheth, and growth up; in the evening it is cut down, and withereth...

For all our days are passed away in thy wrath: *we spend our years as a tale that is told.*

The days of our years are threescore years and ten; and if by reason of strength they be fourscore years, yet is their strength labor and sorrow; *for it is soon cut off, and we fly away*...

So teach us to number our days, that we may apply our hearts unto wisdom...

O satisfy us early with thy mercy; that we may rejoice and be glad all our days...

Let thy work appear unto thy servants, and thy glory unto their children.

And let the beauty of the LORD our God be upon us: and establish thou the work of our hands upon us; yea, the work of our hands establish thou it.

...and now,

it is your turn to recall—

—as far back as you can remember!

LaVergne, TN USA
25 August 2010
194506LV00004B/16/A